First World War
and Army of Occupation
War Diary
France, Belgium and Germany

36 DIVISION
Divisional Troops
Royal Irish Rifles
16th Battalion Pioneers
1 October 1915 - 31 March 1919

WO95/2498/2

The Naval & Military Press Ltd
www.nmarchive.com
Published in association with The National Archives

Published by

The Naval & Military Press Ltd

Unit 10 Ridgewood Industrial Park,

Uckfield, East Sussex,

TN22 5QE England

Tel: +44 (0) 1825 749494

www.naval-military-press.com

www.nmarchive.com

This diary has been reprinted in facsimile from the original. Any imperfections are inevitably reproduced and the quality may fall short of modern type and cartographic standards.

© Crown Copyright
Images reproduced by permission of The National Archives, London, England, 2015.

Contents

Document type	Place/Title	Date From	Date To
Heading	WO95/2498/2 16th Battalion Royal Irish Rifles (Pioneers).		
Heading	36th Division Divl Troops 16th Bn Roy. Irish Rif. (Pioneers) Oct-1915-Apr 1919 Box 2498.		
Heading	36th Divisional Pioneers. 1/16th Battalion Royal Irish Rifles (Pioneers) July 1916:		
War Diary	Aveluy.	01/07/1916	01/07/1916
War Diary	Thiepval.	02/07/1916	04/07/1916
War Diary	Aveluy Thiepval.	05/07/1916	05/07/1916
War Diary	Thiepval.	06/07/1916	06/07/1916
War Diary	Aveluy Thiepval.	07/07/1916	07/07/1916
War Diary	Thiepval.	07/07/1916	24/07/1916
War Diary	Neuve Eglise District.	27/07/1916	27/07/1916
War Diary	Opposite Enemy at Messines.	30/07/1916	31/07/1916
Heading	30th Div 16th R. Irish Rifle Vol I Pioneers 121/7935 Oct 15-Apr 19.		
War Diary	Bordon.	01/10/1915	03/10/1915
War Diary	Villers Bocage.	04/10/1915	11/10/1915
War Diary	Raincheval.	12/10/1915	22/10/1915
Heading	16th R. Irish Rifles Vol 2 Pioneers.		
War Diary	Raincheval.	01/11/1915	19/11/1915
War Diary	Raincheval.	06/12/1915	29/12/1915
Heading	16 R H Rif 36 Div Vol 3 Pioneers Feb.		
War Diary	Candas.	01/01/1916	21/01/1916
War Diary	Raincheval.	22/01/1916	20/03/1916
War Diary	Raincheval.	01/03/1916	25/03/1916
War Diary	Acheux-Candas.	01/05/1916	31/05/1916
War Diary	Aveluy Wood	31/05/1916	31/05/1916
Heading	36th Divisional Pioneers 1/16th Battalion Royal Irish Rifles (Pioneers) June 1916.		
War Diary	Aveluy.	01/06/1916	23/06/1916
War Diary	Aveluy & Thiepval.	23/06/1916	30/06/1916
War Diary	Bulford Camp Near (front S Of) Neuve Eglise.	01/08/1916	17/08/1916
War Diary	T. 28. D.	18/08/1916	31/08/1916
War Diary		01/09/1916	30/09/1916
War Diary	Sheet. 28. S.W T.28.b.9.3.	04/09/1916	05/09/1916
War Diary	T.22.d.4.4	06/09/1916	26/09/1916
War Diary	Divisional Area.	01/10/1916	31/10/1916
War Diary	M.35.d.7.9.	04/10/1916	16/10/1916
War Diary	36th Divisional Area.	01/11/1916	30/11/1916
War Diary		01/11/1916	29/11/1916
War Diary	Divisional Area.	01/12/1916	31/12/1916
War Diary		06/12/1916	29/12/1916
War Diary		21/12/1916	21/12/1916
Miscellaneous	D.A.G., Base.	04/02/1917	04/02/1917
War Diary		01/01/1917	31/01/1917
War Diary		19/01/1917	28/02/1917
War Diary		01/02/1917	31/03/1917
War Diary		12/03/1917	26/03/1917
War Diary	36th Divisional Farm Cwvtschaete-Messines Sector.	01/04/1917	30/04/1917

War Diary		01/04/1917	30/04/1917
War Diary		14/04/1917	27/04/1917
War Diary		03/04/1917	30/04/1917
War Diary		19/04/1917	19/04/1917
War Diary	36th Division Front (Wytschaete-Messines Sector).	01/05/1917	30/05/1917
War Diary		07/05/1917	07/05/1917
War Diary		06/05/1917	24/05/1917
War Diary		01/05/1917	31/05/1917
War Diary	36th Divisional Front (Wytschaete-Messines Sector) (Sheet 28 S.W.).	01/06/1917	07/06/1917
War Diary	36th Divisional Front. (Wytschaete-Messines Sector).	07/06/1917	28/06/1917
War Diary	36th Divisional Front (Wytschaete-Messine Sector).	26/06/1917	30/06/1917
War Diary		05/06/1917	27/06/1917
War Diary		07/06/1917	27/06/1917
War Diary	Back Area.	01/07/1917	11/07/1917
War Diary	Ypres Sector.	12/07/1917	22/07/1917
War Diary	Forward Area.	23/07/1917	25/07/1917
War Diary	Ypres Sector.	26/07/1917	31/07/1917
War Diary	Ypres Sector.	07/07/1917	19/07/1917
War Diary	Ypres Sector.	06/07/1917	04/08/1917
War Diary	Ypres Front.	05/08/1917	28/08/1917
War Diary	Ypres Front. (St Julien Sector).	29/08/1917	31/08/1917
War Diary		01/08/1917	27/08/1917
War Diary		01/08/1917	30/08/1917
Miscellaneous	Narrative of part taken by 16th Bn. Roy. IR. Rifs. (P). (less one Coy.) during Operations on the 16th. August. 1917.	16/08/1917	16/08/1917
War Diary	Ypres Sector.	01/09/1917	27/09/1917
War Diary	Havrincourt Front (Somme).	28/09/1917	30/09/1917
War Diary		04/09/1917	26/09/1917
War Diary		05/09/1917	17/09/1917
War Diary		14/09/1917	24/09/1917
War Diary	Havrincourt Front Somme.	01/10/1917	31/10/1917
War Diary		01/10/1917	25/10/1917
War Diary		04/10/1917	28/10/1917
War Diary		27/10/1917	27/10/1917
War Diary		08/10/1917	21/10/1917
War Diary	Havrincourt Front. Ref. Sheet. 57c. France. S.E & N.E.	01/11/1917	19/11/1917
War Diary	Cambrai Front. (Ribecourt Sector).	20/11/1917	20/11/1917
War Diary	Ribecourt Sector.	21/11/1917	24/11/1917
War Diary	Moeuvres Sector.	24/11/1917	01/12/1917
War Diary		04/11/1917	20/11/1917
War Diary		02/11/1917	13/11/1917
War Diary		01/11/1917	28/11/1917
War Diary	Cambrai Front.	01/12/1917	19/01/1918
War Diary	St Quentin Front.	19/01/1918	31/01/1918
War Diary	36th Div Front St. Quentin Sector.	01/02/1918	28/02/1918
Heading	36th Divisional Pioneers 16th Battalion Royal Irish Rifles. March 1918.		
War Diary		01/03/1918	31/03/1918
Heading	36th Divisional Pioneers 1/16th Battalion Royal Irish Rifles (Pioneers) April 1918.		
War Diary	36th Divisional Front Ypres Sector.	01/04/1918	30/04/1918
War Diary		07/04/1918	28/04/1918
War Diary	Ypres Front. 36th Divn. Sector.	01/05/1918	01/06/1918
War Diary	36th Div Corps. II Reserve.	02/06/1918	08/06/1918

War Diary		06/06/1918	30/06/1918
War Diary	II Corps Reserce. Proven.	01/07/1918	01/07/1918
War Diary	XVI. Trench Corps Reserve	02/07/1918	03/07/1918
War Diary	St Marie Cappel Area.	04/07/1918	06/07/1918
War Diary	X Corps St Jans Cappel Sector.	07/07/1918	18/07/1918
War Diary		16/07/1918	22/07/1918
War Diary	St Jans Cappel Sector.	23/07/1918	30/07/1918
Miscellaneous	36th Divn. G.	02/09/1918	02/09/1918
War Diary	St Jans Cappel Sector.	01/08/1918	12/08/1918
War Diary		03/08/1918	30/09/1918
Operation(al) Order(s)	Operation Order No. 40.		
War Diary		01/10/1918	31/10/1918
Miscellaneous	Casualties during October.		
War Diary	Mouscron (Sheet 29/S 22.	01/11/1918	09/11/1918
War Diary	Autryve (29/V8d).	10/11/1918	16/11/1918
War Diary	Mouscron (29/S22).	18/11/1918	30/11/1918
War Diary	Mouscron.	01/12/1918	31/12/1918
Miscellaneous	Group 1. 107th Infantry Brigade Education Return.		
Miscellaneous	107th Bde No. G 439 App II.	28/01/1919	28/01/1919
War Diary	Mouscron (Belgium) (Sheet 29/S 22).	00/01/1919	00/01/1919
War Diary	Mouscron Belgium.	01/02/1919	31/03/1919
War Diary	Mouscron Belgium.	00/04/1919	00/04/1919

WO95/2498/2
16th Battalion Royal Irish Rifles
(Pioneers)

36TH DIVISION
DIVL TROOPS

16TH BN ROY. IRISH RIF.
(PIONEERS)
OCT-1915- APR 1919

Box 2498

36th Divisional Pioneers.

1/16th BATTALION

ROYAL IRISH RIFLES (Pioneers)

JULY 1916::

WAR DIARY
INTELLIGENCE SUMMARY. 16th R.I. Rif. (Pioneers)

July 1916.

Place	Date	Hour	Summary of Events and Information	Remarks
AVELUY	1st	5.30 A.M.	Moved to our place of assembly, starting an hour early, as I knew the enemy would probably know our hour of attack & I wished to avoid their custom fire. Return to assemble at LANCASHIRE Dump, but no shelter there & road being heavily shelled, so took M.O. to some old trenches had found by a reconnaissance previous night, about 200 x 10 of part named left Pioneer under a shelter (until previous night) at LANCASHIRE Dump).	
	6 a.m.		The most tremendous bombardment both replies to by enemy; owing to precautions mentioned in last para, had no casualties.	
	7.30		Other charged. It was very difficult to see owing to smoke & burst & mist, but we were not fathered, & they were from me 1st & 2nd lines of trenches.	
	8.40		Sent No 1 Coy to HAMEL to repair St PIERRE – DIVION Rd. No 2 to cut trench across No Mans Land from Nos 5 Cop to enemy 1st line. No 3 found road in possession of enemy to Command MR 1st line at HAMEL, & carrying party to bring in wounded B.& R.I. Rif. Who were lying in numbers heavy fire. Though in about 60 h 70, but by 12 noon in abouts & No 2 made several most billowed efforts to cut the trench required, but gave them down as very W.R. cop each time. But about 20 men before abandoning all night. I thought No 3 Cof. to reinforce No 2. About 9 P.M. as they were drawing...	

WAR DIARY
INTELLIGENCE SUMMARY

Army Form C. 2118.

16th R.I.R. Diy (Morning) Sheet 2 (2)

July 1916

Place	Date	Hour	Summary of Events and Information	Remarks and references to Appendices
THIEPVAL	2nd	9 AM	We heard at intervals not: our men retreated from enemy 1st line. Capt. Chas. Cherril great calmness & methody still in helping to make arrangements for holding our 1st line. But the enemy shewed attack. All THIEPVAL WOOD was now under very heavy shell fire, & the scene was beyond description.	
	2nd	2 PM	Lt. Maventy & 20 men took part in the highly successful attack of the 107th & 108th R.I.R. This number of enemy & covered such on fire 3 times to bring up ammunition was highly reported on by G.O.C. 107th Inf. Bde. Lt. Maventy was one of the 73 who went with him. 1/Lt McDowan organised & commanded the bombers most successfully.	
		6 PM	Retired to our bivouac in AVELUY. 3rd Bn. had not been relieved in afternoon	
	3rd		No 3 Coy. to another bivouac nr: to T Railway at THIEPVAL to cut trenches across no man's land for 49 & 50 Bde. No 3 Coy. succeeded in cutting these trenches but with cover lines as the trench was cut. 2nd Lt Cole killed while most gallantly supervising a part of the French Railway surveyed by shells. Several casualties among our Railway Party not having a fright men.	
	4th		The trench across no man's land was destroyed by shell fire, we cut it again in night	

Army Form C. 2118.

WAR DIARY
or
INTELLIGENCE SUMMARY.
(Erase heading not required.)

16th O.O: Rif (Pursue). Part 3

July 1916

Place	Date	Hour	Summary of Events and Information	Remarks and references to Appendices
AVELUY THIEPVAL	5th	2.30 p.m.	The enemy opened a rather intense bombardment on AVELUY WOOD. The hours I had spent experimenting [much of them during the first] 2½ hours. We noticed that over 2000 shells of all sorts fell in & around our bivouacs in 2½ hours. The two were marked down. The other 300 & other shellers were always, as were most of our other branches, though enough - altho' several of the dug outs we had built were blown in, we had only 4 casualties. There were one a Lance B 6", 3" & shrapnel within a few feet of the HQ dug shelter, but fortunately no direct hit. That night we went down to No Man's Land from about Sap 7 in THIEPVAL & buried & identified a chaplain on a bank, which another Pioneer Party had been unable to dig. We made (on) improvised only being about a dozen men.	
THIEPVAL	6th	4 p.m.	We continued & deepened trench during previous night, as it had been shelled to day by enemy shell fire. Lieut Cave & another Pioneer Bt. were told off to assist us, but did not materialise except for a few minutes. We remained under heavy shell fire from 9 p.m. to 2 a.m. when heavy low hurdy we (?) the order to retire from 14th Bt. RB. 2. 2. Lt Marwill while uncovering with another Officer was wounded by shrapnel, & orders had to come. We then drew non uniforms up, so 2. Lt Marwill went back & fetched him in	
AVELUY THIEPVAL	7th		The Brench Railway having been much damaged by shell fire, we turned out to repair it. Lt McLellan who was in charge after the death of L.Cple. directing proceedings, & Sinnon my men having been up & night in trenches were much exhausted, so I went	

Army Form C. 2118.

WAR DIARY
or
INTELLIGENCE SUMMARY.
(Erase heading not required.)

15th N.Y. N.F. (Monins)

July 1916.

Place	Date	Hour	Summary of Events and Information	Remarks and references to Appendices
THIEPVAL	7th		15th Bn. Hq at PAISLEY. I got a mild N/S, the 4 mile had suren, & Vedu Ave I was in parts up to my waist in water	
	8th	3 p.m.	Band marching & carrying ammunition	
			Orders came to return to HARPONVILLE, arrived late that night	
	10th	6 A.m.	Marched from HARPONVILLE to BEAUVAL, billeted there	
	11th	4 A.m.	— — BEAUVAL to BERNAVILLE — —	
	12th	2:30 A.m.	— — BERNAVILLE to CONTEVILLE, entrained there at 8:30 A.m., arr CONTEVILLE	
		1:30 P.M.	marched to BLARINGHAM	
	13th	11 A.M.	marched to MOULLE	
	[19th 20th 18th]		3 days stormy & cleaning up. The men much exhausted. Capt. Mure broke down from overstrain & has gone home	
	21st	10 A.m.	Marched to VOLKERINCKHOVE, witnessed explosion of our ammunition dumps at AUDRUICQ	
	22nd	9 A.	Marched to WINNEZEELE via NOORDPEENE & WEMAERS. Billeted there, 2nd Lt Smith Whedon & was invalided	
	23rd	8:30 A.m	Marched to BEAUVOORDE, 2 miles SW of STEENVOORDE, camped in Belgian border	
	24th	8:30 A.m	Marched to a field on a hill about 2½ miles from BAILLEUL, found some dilapidated sanitary huts from a Bn & billeted these. & camped	

Army Form C. 2118.

WAR DIARY
or
INTELLIGENCE SUMMARY. 16th R.I.R. Nij. (R.)

(Erase heading not required.)

Title pages July 1916

Place	Date	Hour	Summary of Events and Information	Remarks and references to Appendices
Neuve EGLISE District	27th		Marched to Pt. 14 on map for work in trenches. Camped there. Up to date during Somme operations, 2nd (Moving) Offnrs. Killed 2, W. Offrs. & 9 men. (latter accidentally) wounded 2 offrs & men Dumour (D.v.) & Lt Bullum, injured Capt. Allen & Groves. In the above Capt. O'Brien, Knox, Platt, & Groves, 2 Lt. Watts. constitute any force 18 J., & first enabler 100 men immobilised. Major Antrobus was Liaison Officer to Avreley Wood during operations. 2nd Lt Watts special turn to Div. 24 Lt Watts injured returns to D.A. Left Hd. Qtrs. marched to Refit Pont Fm about 2 miles East, under Capt. Chase. Camped there. No 1. C.J. Sullied Works at work, one man wounded.	
Onrish Camp (at) MESSINES	30th 31st			

John Leadinghend
Col. 16 R.I.R. Nij. (R).

16th R. Ir. Rif. Vol I
Pioneers

121/7935

Oct '15 / Ap '19

36th Div

Confidential

Army Form C. 2118.

038/7/49

WAR DIARY
or
INTELLIGENCE SUMMARY. 16th R.I.Rif. (Pioneers)

October 1915

(Erase heading not required.)

Place	Date	Hour	Summary of Events and Information	Remarks and references to Appendices
Boulogne	1/10/15		Left Southampton 7 PM to S'hampton, no ships, spent all night on the pier.	
	2/10/15		Sailed in a ferry boat EMPRESS QUEEN to HAVRE, arr 10 am after midnight	
	3/10/15	1.30 AM	Arr 1.30 AM, entrained to LONGEAU, arr 7 PM, marched to VILLERS BOCAGE arr midnight owing to lack of transport, had to leave tools behind, received them next day	
VILLERS BOCAGE	Oct 4 – 11th		Sent party of carpenters to fix up Divl HQ, built road fr the 2d Cavalry Divn Hqrs	
RAINCHEVAL	Oct 12		Marched to RAINCHEVAL & camped there, started next day # on the "Army Line," joining the line from a point 1600x SE of TOUT ENCOURT, leaving the French line, thence N to CREFTAL WOOD, & 2 works near RAINCHEVAL – VAUCHELLES Rd.	
		On 12th	We saw our first engagement, an aeroplane fight, & three (Allies) enveloped during our stay. RAINCHEVAL is about 7 miles W of the firing line at that time	
	Oct 13th		Our men into billets, & started making improvements in the village, which was in a shocking sanitary state, & being right down in a hollow, was practically a swamp. Roads which ran thro' & contained encampments, filth, horses, chunks worms etc.	
	Oct 14 Oct 15 Oct 18		Carried on the "Army Line" HqQ Hdqrs in TOUTENCOURT under Major Herman 16/Nth My (P1) No 2 Coy (Capt Platt) to VIGNACOURT to our shown the three lines & make gabions hurdles & fascines (nom les trenchons)	
	Oct 21 Oct 22		Inspected by Lieutenant Officer 3rd Army. Marched down to our position to the firing line, & attached them to 9th Sc Rifles (Pioneers), who were extremely keen in instructing our men to our putting up hurdles, were engrossments in front of our fire trenches.	

16th R. Irish Rifles
Vol 2
Pioneers.

36

"Confidential"

Army Form C. 2118.

WAR DIARY
or
INTELLIGENCE SUMMARY. 16 K.R.R. Rifles (Pioneers)

(Erase heading not required.)

November 1915

Place	Date	Hour	Summary of Events and Information	Remarks and references to Appendices
RAINNEVAL	Nov 3		Opening of Regimental Canteen & Army & Reading Room.	
	Nov 4		Inspection by M.G.C. Gen'l in his Q.L.I.	
	Nov 6		No Coy A⁺⁺ R E placed under Capt⁺. Platt at VIGNACOURT	
			R E Signalling Cpt. placed under charge of Capt⁺ Shepperd Cmd. No 1 Coy, for instruction. He then took over the defence of ARQUEVES in addition to our other works. These defences had been started by A.R.E. but had to be reconstructed.	
			Owing to the heavy rains following severe frost, a double tier of revetment became necessary in trenches, & dug outs required for heavier uprights than he could obtain.	
	Nov 19		Half of No 1 Coy. under Lt. Somerfield to MARIEUX, & started timber work in the Forest there.	
			Inspection by Div A.D.M.S.	

J. Mackintosh Col.
Comd⁺ 16 K.R.R. Rif. (Pioneers)

Confidential

Army Form C. 2118.

WAR DIARY
or
INTELLIGENCE SUMMARY.

(Erase heading not required.)

December 1915   1st R.O? Rifles (Princess)

Place	Date	Hour	Summary of Events and Information	Remarks and references to Appendices
RAINNEUVAL	6th		Three young officers with the battn. no knowledge of Engineering or Surveying. Sent me to reinforce us. We have 14 highly trained Pioneer Officers working more or less for a chance to come out.	
	13th		No 3 Platoon as an C.P. part of No 1 C.P. proceeds to FLESELLES, under 2/Lt. Darling, they are to build a large ammunition shed with cement foundation, & make 3 metalled roads leading to & from it, each 400 x long.	
	18th		No 1 Platoon filled No 3.	
	24th		2nd platoon of No 4 C.P. from TOUTENCOURT to MENTIERES for 2 weeks quarrying	
	27th		One remaining Platoon of No 1 C.P. to FLESELLES	
	28th		Nos 2 & 3 Coys & No 4 Coy. to CANDAS to build a railway 17 miles long from CANDAS through BEAUVAL — PUCHEVILLERS — RAINCHEVAL to ACHEUX. H?q? & No 2 C.P. at BEAUVAL, No 3 C.P. at FIENVILLERS, & No 4 C.P. at CANDAS. While these Coys were marching out, 4 German Planes made a raid & dropped 8 bombs no far from them, arriving Woriely at the aerodrome. There were attacked and driven off by French Planes.	
	29th		Started the Railway from CANDAS, making a terminal station there	

[signature]

16 R & RB
36D3
Vol 3
PIONEERS Feb.

Confidential.

Army Form C. 2118.

16th RT. Rif (Pioneers)

WAR DIARY
or
INTELLIGENCE SUMMARY.
(Erase heading not required.)

Instructions regarding War Diaries and Intelligence Summaries are contained in F.S. Regs., Part II. and the Staff Manual respectively. Title pages will be prepared in manuscript.

January 1916

Place	Date	Hour	Summary of Events and Information	Remarks and references to Appendices
CANDAS	1st		Carried on with the Railway at the almost unprecedented rate of about 1100 yards of chal per day, this including a dump.	
	21st		A Railway accident, owing to having necessarily to run heavy trains over unballasted steel, 2 men were killed & 13 wounded. Genl Allenby (the army cmdr) paid our Bn (and general sanction after the smash).	
RAINCHEVAL 22nd			Hd Qrs move to RAINCHEVAL, with 2no. H and 2 Coys., no 3 Coy. remaining at CANDAS for packing & ballasting. Visit by Lord Derwent & Sir James Remy. No 1 Coy. moved from FLESELLES to ACHEUX, where they started the Terminal Station at that end.	
			The following Infantry Regts sent detachments to work on the Railway, with supervision during their month. R. Inniskilling Fus (2 offs.), 4th S. Lancs Rgt.; 4th K.O.Rgt (R. Lancs) A.S.C. Highlanders, & a Pike 16/(Leinsters, 12th D.Y.Rif (S.W.B.), Devonshire Rgt. The Survey & Location was carried out by 2/Lts. Minnin & Slater, Capt(?) (Act) Allen, assisted by Capt Jewell. General Supervision over the Engineering work, 2/Lt Brown had all the land crossings. Capt Watts was in charge of the bulk of the Plate laying, Capt. Chase of the ballasting & following & straightening.	
	31st		CO summoned to G Hqr for a conference on Pioneer Training & Organisation	

John Lenkins(?) Col 16 RTR Rif (Pi)

Confidential

16th Royal Irish Rifles (Pioneers)

February 1916

Army Form C. 2118.

WAR DIARY
or
INTELLIGENCE SUMMARY.
(Erase heading not required.)

Instructions regarding War Diaries and Intelligence Summaries are contained in F.S. Regs., Part II. and the Staff Manual respectively. Title pages will be prepared in manuscript.

Place	Date	Hour	Summary of Events and Information	Remarks and references to Appendices
RAINCHEVAL	1st		Bn. HQrs at RAINCHEVAL with Nos 2 and 4 Coys to finish up the laying of the steel of the line. No 1 Coy. at ACHEUX to build the terminus & sidings there, and also a large cement tank. No 3 Coy. performed similar works at the Other terminus — CANDAS.	
	13th		Lt Col Leader sent for to GHQ and sent on a special mission, returning to Bn. 27th April.	
	18th		Final spike driven in, and steel completed near Belle Eglise Farm. No 4 Coy. started on the station and sidings there. No 2 Coy. continued ballasting and rectifying the work, but no casualties. No 1 Coy. shelled several times during the month, but no casualties	

John Leader Lt Col
Comdg 16 R.I.Rif (P)

OB/1329

March 1916.

Army Form C. 2118.

WAR DIARY
or
INTELLIGENCE SUMMARY.
(Erase heading not required.)

16/ R.E. Rifles (Pioneers)

Place	Date	Hour	Summary of Events and Information	Remarks and references to Appendices
RAINCHEVAL	1st		Line continued raising the slacks & & driving new sidings. Owing to manpower part of line, notably by PUCHVILLERS, line sank very considerably.	
	2nd		Major Bowen transferred to 14th R.E. Rfs (Young Bridging) to command them.	
	9th		Div. having been transferred from 3rd to 4th Army, a letter from G.O.C. 3rd Army to O.C. 16th R.E. Rfs (P) expressing regret at losing the services of the Batt. also a letter from G.H.Q. to R.E. Rfs. appreciating work of the Batt. and stating that their services would be represented to higher authority.	
	11th			
	20th		BELLE EGLISE Station finished; arrival of an R.T.O. for whom an office had to be built. Line opened to traffic; heavy trains loaded with munitions, supplies & troops began to arrive at short intervals.	
			Entertainments this month (afternoons from 4 p.m. to 8:30 p.m.) one regiment: 3 days boxing Tournament; 4 days Cinema Show; 3 days Divisional "Follies"; amateur Concert & Regt. Minstrel Troupe.	

R Gardner Major
16/R.E. Rfles (P)

Confidential

March 1916

16th R. Irish Rif (Pioneers)   Army Form C. 2118.

WAR DIARY
or
INTELLIGENCE SUMMARY.

Place	Date	Hour	Summary of Events and Information	Remarks and references to Appendices
RAINNEVAL	1st		Line continued, leaving the Clerk & adding new sidings. Being to transport our part of line, mostly by PUCHEVILLERS, line used very considerably.	
	2nd		Major Bragmann transferred to 14th N.I. Rif (Young Citizens) to command them.	
	9th		Bn. having been transferred from 3rd to 4th Army, a letter from C.S. 3rd Army to O.C. 16th N.I. Rif (P) received right at losing the Division & the 15th, also	
	11th		a letter from 'A' Coy to R.C.S. & apprenticing work of the 15th, and stating that their Service would be represented to higher authority.	
	28th		Rille Ophir Station finished, around 3 am RTO for whom an Office had to be built. Line opened to TRAFFIC, & from hour trains travel with munitions, supplies, & troops begin to arrive at short intervals.	
			Entertainments this month (after dinner from 7 P.M. to 8.30 P.M.) were frequent. 3 days boxing tournament, 4 days Cinema show, 3 days "Gos & Follies" finding Concert, & Pipe & Minstrel troupe.	

WAR DIARY or INTELLIGENCE SUMMARY

Army Form C. 2118.

16th R.I. Rgt (Pioneers)
XXXVI

16 R I Rgt
Vol 5

April 1916

Place	Date	Hour	Summary of Events and Information	Remarks and references to Appendices
Raincheval			The following officers were extra-regimentally employed during the month:—	

Capt Jewell — In charge CANDAS Terminal Stn & the new Diamond Crossings & intermediate sidings, also 7½ to 12½ mile sect of Gd Rly from CANDAS — RUBEL, & supervising various Reviews.

Capt M. Shepard — In charge Const. ROSEL to PUCHEVILLERS, & supt working parties, relieved by Lt Gibson

Capt Mott — In charge all buildings & plant horses, platforms etc. along the Line

Lt Billing — In charge picture pumps along the Line.

Lt W. Slater — Only started trying work for the Divl. I.E. 5.20.4., from 10th instbll. the steel shelters along the Line.

Lt Woburn — Reached via his opened studies to Capt Jewell on 20th, & proceeded to MARTINSART to fight & build shelters for the Div Arty Hdqrs.

The M.G. during the month completed the junction at BELLE-EGLISE with 4 sidings, finished the parking & ballasting, & re-ballasted in all sharply places. They added several new sidings along the line, & put up the buildings, Examination & repair pits, coal banks etc. They also built 2 concrete airroom pillars tanks, & at CANDAS, & one at ACHEUX, to provide water for engines.

Two detachments, each under an Officer, were sent each week for a tour of duty at the Trenches (One Mr supplied instruments & fighting near YPRES-out with the 15th and 17th Brigs. (Gen Green, Barton, Jameson, choir), with the 10th WYWLFs in front (1st to 17th Nov.), & with the 4th Divn two (Lt Longmore), The latter was hit by shrapnel on his left shoulder at Mosni Clown, & been attended to 108 RAR with party of 30 Pioneers to do the wiring on Mine Road, the supplying, & a small MG fortements.

Mahrshers Lt
Col 16 R.I. Rgt (Pioneers)

16th R.I.R. (Pioneers)

WAR DIARY
INTELLIGENCE SUMMARY

Month: May 1916

Vol 6

Place	Date	Hour	Summary of Events and Information	Remarks and references to Appendices
ACHEUX – CANDAS	1st		Work on Railway continued. New sidings & crossings, laying the plank through the marsh near ROSEL, extending 9 Vehl Tanks, Building platforms & offices. HQ. Cd. CANDAS to PUCHEVILLERS, Hd. 3 Coy PUCHEVILLERS. — ACHEUX. Detachment with 16th R.I.R. heavily bombarded, but only 2 casualties, 1 M.E. wounded.	
	2nd		Inv. Morris & 50 men with 108 A.T. Coy R.E. working on front of our 1st line. Cement garments, dug outs etc.	
		11.40	Nos 2 & 4 Coys proceed to Trenches today for work on THIEPVAL with 9 / 1st Army. 2/Lt Waters taken for special work under G.O.C. 1st Army. Presents 2nd Lt. Brown (Riles) as Engineer attached to the Workshop of the Division. Latter has being taken over management & maintenance of Trench Railway, provides carpenters to Divn HQrs. No 2 Coy takes over Trench Railway, 2 & 4 Coys the Trench Railway & digging from our 1st line to running enemy line.	
		12.40	Capt. Powell injured by fall from his horse & sent to England, Lt Alister was sent to Q.H. in England. Capt. Allen injured & sent to Home on 15.5.16	
	3rd		Railway finished. Whole Bn concentrates in AVELUY WOOD, employed making dug outs for 9th Divn at THIEPVAL and in front of HAMEL, working in front of our 1st line. Making accessory trenches in THIEPVAL, making inroads, camouflage, 90 m. on management, main tunnel of the Trench Railway, the Slide for special Trench Tramway track under 9 Divn, & 1st Corps whole waggon as supplies by this Battn.	
AVELUY WOOD				

Cavalry 16 R.I. Reg. Pl.

36th Divisional Pioneers

1/16th BATTALION

ROYAL IRISH RIFLES

(Pioneers)

JUNE 1916

WAR DIARY or INTELLIGENCE SUMMARY

Army Form C. 2118.

16th Bn R J Rif (Pioneers)

XXXVI Division

June 1916

Place	Date	Hour	Summary of Events and Information	Remarks and references to Appendices
AVELUY	1st		Rem a while O/R marched from RAINCHEVAL to AVELUY WOOD, & from a third time	
"	2nd	2.45AM	Enemy heavily bombarded AVELUY WOOD, our casualties 2 killed 4 wounded. Men properly calm & steady	
"	3rd		All available men turned on to cut out lumber to refix to, in case of further bombardments. Started on trench in THIEPVAL. These consisted chiefly in building assembly trenches, & communication trenches (Connaught, Inniskilling, & Seventh Ave) to the 1st line. Trench mortar emplacements in WHITCHURCH Street, Bomb Stores & Ration Stores in ROSS Street, 1000 yards of Trench Tramway along Speyside, & 400 yards up Paisley Ave, repairs & upkeep of existing lines. Whiling up supplies, building 5 dug outs in Paisley, deepening and from 1st line, making Martinsart – Inglethorpe Road, building a big dugout in Paisley, deepening work at Gen H.Q. in ELGIN, building road across AUTHUILE marsh with fascines, building shelters for Gen & helping 1st Line & Thiepval Garrison Admin H.Q. & these minor duties. We lost about 30 men in doing this, 20 casualties on special work at Thiepval, 10 men with Capt N.S. at GORDON Castle, 2 NCO 50 men at HAMEL lumber dumps turned by C.R.E. about 5 have Mechanisat from to Battle, were commenced on 19th inst, & NCOs & men worked to finish, 6 hours 14 hours a day work in 2 shifts, 1 NCO & 12 by day	
	13th		by night returning for meals to the work each night. Capt Green mentioned in dispatches LONDON GAZETTE of this date.	
	15th		Montauban & bymm to 23rd.	
	16th		Montauban bymm, many replies, Conveying a few shells into AVELUY. We went on with our work, all men that can be spared cut, deepen & breve old trenches. Recently continuous rain & butter wet.	

Army Form C. 2118.

WAR DIARY
or
INTELLIGENCE SUMMARY. 16th N.Y. N.G. (Pioneers)

(Erase heading not required.)

Instructions regarding War Diaries and Intelligence Summaries are contained in F. S. Regs., Part II. and the Staff Manual respectively. Title pages will be prepared in manuscript.

June 23rd to 30th

Place	Date	Hour	Summary of Events and Information	Remarks and references to Appendices
AVELUY to THIEPVAL	23rd to 30th		During the bombardment, we continued our works in THIEPVAL, & about 150 men assisting up the mothers & ammunition & supplies to the front line. We had several men during this period on the enemy kept up a constant fire. A most favorable report on the Battn work in a raid from G.O.C. 108th A.I.	
	30th		Completed all engineering works required. Lost 16 men on the enemy cutting wire heavily active in the last 24 hours.	

John Ward Lt Col
comdt 16 N.Y. N.G. (Pioneers)

Confidential

OR/1/461

Shut 1
16th R.I.R. 2nd Ny (Pioneers) Vol 9

Army Form C. 2118.

WAR DIARY
or
INTELLIGENCE SUMMARY.
(Erase heading not required.)

Instructions regarding War Diaries and Intelligence Summaries are contained in F. S. Regs., Part II. and the Staff Manual respectively. Title pages will be prepared in manuscript.

Army Form C. 2118.

Place	Date	Hour	Summary of Events and Information	Remarks and references to Appendices
BULFORD Camp (Pat S A) NEUVE EGLISE	1st		Continued work in Trenches. Shells fairly continually, but only 1 man wounded.	
			getting little down ROUND PETIT PONT Farm.	
	4th		Several shells fell close to No 3 Coys Barn - billet, & two pitched in it, killing all their mules, & wounding	
			Cpl Cowles charge. Also damaged several rifles & equipment, & started a fire which destroyed a considerable amount	
			of S.A.A.	
	6th		Trouble with MMG O/s of Div to find billets for the 2 Coys at Bulfort — during the front, found quite a lost barn	
			called "Grande Munque Farm" about 2000 yards behind our front line, which will hold 300 men.	
	7th		Moved to a point S of Petit Pont Fm T 25 D. Camped there	
	8th		Col Losler evacuated to No. 12 C.C.S.	
	9th		No. 4 Coy issues transferred from Salvage car. his to 14 AS Ferries, Kings barns	
			IRIR O/C 14th R.I.R. reporting to & assumes Command of Bn	
	10th		Party 2 NCOS & 14 O.R to St. Omer for defaulters exercises.	
	12th		Major Lees acting during higher.	
	13th		4 NCOs & 34 O.R. report to 145th Munceering Coy.	
	14th 15th 16th 17th		Nothing unusual	
			2 NCos 44 O.R. detailed to represent O.C. 16th Bear Munceering on Report on Billets 83 Corps round General expressed Satisfaction of work.	

Signed Lewis Esmonde
O.C. 16th R.I.R.(P)

Confidential   16th R.I. Rifles (P)   Sheet 2.

Army Form C. 2118.

WAR DIARY
or
INTELLIGENCE SUMMARY.
(Erase heading not required.)

Place	Date	Hour	Summary of Events and Information	Remarks and references to Appendices
T.28.D	18th		Lewis gun attacks to Selves. 1 Off, 2 Regs. 10mm. Report of Lewis Gun Det. at Selves nery excellent.	
	19th		Without previous warning our artillery started bombardment. Several retaliations 8 killed 2 men 8 wounded 3 of No 2. Coy. 3 men wounded No 3. Cy. 1 stunned since died.	
	20th 21st 22nd		Nothing unusual	
	23rd		3 N.C.O.'s & 33 men to Ste Phepare Emplacement 4 M.B.	
	24th		Sentry No 3. challenging another man No 3. getting no reply. Bayonetted him unconscious to everyone.	
	25th 26th		No 1. Cy. Shelled at Usher. No casualties	
	27th		All remainder of Coy. carrying gas cylinders to front trenches at Night	
	28th		Ditto	
	29th		Waited to prepare for gas attack of tomorrow.	
	30/31		Gas attack 1.30 am. Artillery Bombardment & Raid. Raiders wiped out.	
	31st		No 1. Cy. Shelled on way to trench usher. General retaliation all day by enemy. Small Gas attack on Boesinghe.	

C. H. Maxwell Major
O.C. 16th I.R.R (P)

Army Form C. 2118/0

WO/95

CONFIDENTIAL.

Instructions regarding War Diaries and Intelligence Summaries are contained in F.S. Regs., Part II. and the Staff Manual respectively. Title pages will be prepared in manuscript.

WAR DIARY
or
INTELLIGENCE SUMMARY.
(Erase heading not required.)

ORDERLY ROOM No. 08/11/849 Date 2.10.16 IRISH RIFLES (PIONEERS)

16TH ROYAL IRISH RIFS. (PIONEERS)

SEPTEMBER 1916.

Place	Date	Hour	Summary of Events and Information	Remarks and references to Appendices
	1st to 30th		Batts. engaged on Divisional front, constructing & reconnoitring emplacements, revetting & framing communication trenches, work in Reverian gaps, dug-outs, screening, hutting, etc. Horse standings at T.20.C.3.1. Sheet 28. O.W.	
SHEET. 28.S.W. 128.b.9.3.	4th	8.30 p.m.	8 rds of evo 16° shelled - no casualties.	
	5th		Bn.H.Qrs. in evos. 2 & 4 B.HQ. moved to DRANOUTRE.	
T.22.d.4.4.	6th	10 p.m.	No. 3 6° heirs shelled (shrapnel) one man wounded.	
	7th		Vicinity of camp bombed by aeroplane - no damage.	
	10th		Capt. S.W. KNOX rejoined from 20(R) Bn = R.I. RIFS.	
	12th		2/Lieuts. FERGUSON and BLEAKLEY, joined from 17(R) Bn = R.I. RIFS. (DRANOUTRE).	
	22nd	7.30 p.m.	Village shelled; average men wounded in Y en.C.A. Inst.	
	26th		2/Lieut. J.H. CRAIG joined for duty, commissioned from Cadet School G.H.Q.	
			Following parties sent on Courses during the month:-	
			DIVN LEWIS GUN SCHOOL :- 1 Off. 12. O.R. Excellent report on this party received.	
			" 12. O.R.	
			DIVN SCHOOL OF INSTRN :- 1 Off. 2 O.R.	
			2ND ARMY SCHOOL OF INSTRN :- 1 Off. 1 O.R.	

E.C. Heard
Lt. Col.
O.C. 16th R.Ir. Rifs. (P).

1.10.1916.

CONFIDENTIAL.

Army Form C. 2118.

Instructions regarding War Diaries and Intelligence Summaries are contained in F.S. Regs., Part II. and the Staff Manual respectively. Title pages will be prepared in manuscript.

WAR DIARY
or
INTELLIGENCE SUMMARY.
(Erase heading not required.)

16/ ROY. IR. RIFLES (PIONEERS)

OCTOBER. 1916.

Place	Date	Hour	Summary of Events and Information	Remarks and references to Appendices
DIVISIONAL AREA.	1st to 3rd		Battalion engaged on construction of trench mortar emplacements, dug-outs, trench railway. Previous days' revetting, training in drainage of communication trenches, steening, hutting, etc. Horse standings at Sheet 28 S.W., T.20. c.3.1, completed.	
	4th		Experiment on "Intensive" trench digging, carried out – weather improving – result showed normal systems had the advantage.	
M.35.d.7.9.	5th		Batt. Hdqrs. at O.2.6.7. A half of ZO. 5 & 6° moved to camp at M.35.d.7.9.	
	7th		2/Lieuts. FERGUSON and BLEAKLEY,R, left to join 11th ROY. IR. RIFS.	
	10th		Party from ZO.2.6° at work on PICCADILLY AVENUE heavily shelled – one casualty. Party from ZO.26° at work on German mortar emplacements shelled out.	
	11th		Party on heavy railway construction shelled, one casualty.	
	12th		One casualty in night party working on machine gun emplacements.	
	13th		One casualty in night carrying party to CALGARY AVE.	
	16th		Party at work on PICCADILLY AVE. shelled. 2/Lt. McCAY.S. wounded.	
			GENERAL:- Infantry drills, musketry, Lewis gun training, etc., carried out on average. During the month parties were sent on courses to:- II Army school of Instruction. Div.e School of Instruction, and Lewis gun School of Instruction (Army & Div.) and favourable reports received.	

D.J. Moore Lt. Col.
Comdg. 16/R. Ir. Rifs. (P.)

31 . 2 . 16.

Army Form C. 2118.

WAR DIARY
or
INTELLIGENCE SUMMARY.
(Erase heading not required.)

16th R. Ir. Rif. (P)

NOVEMBER - 1916

Instructions regarding War Diaries and Intelligence Summaries are contained in F.S. Regs., Part II. and the Staff Manual respectively. Title pages will be prepared in manuscript.

Place	Date	Hour	Summary of Events and Information	Remarks and references to Appendices
36th DIVISIONAL AREA	1st to 30th		Battalion engaged on construction and repair work, during the entire month, viz:- French Railway - Russian Saps - Making Huts - Digging, draining, levelling, framing and revetting Communication Trenches - Erection Huts - Repairing Huts - Draining Camps.	
	1st		Lt. A. Green rejoined the Battalion.	
	4th		PICCADILLY Communication Trench, where No 2 Coy was employed - nearly shelled.	
	5th		Sunday - Battalion Training - Lewis Gun - Bombing - Practice at Rifle Range &c &c.	
	8th		Owing to heavy rains the DOUVE RIVER rose to such an extent that dug-outs in the neighbourhood and communication trenches were flooded	
	12th		Sunday Training as on 5th	
	14th		2nd Lt. J.A. JOHNSTON rejoined the Batt'n from the BASE DEPOT.	
	19th		Sunday training as on 5th - Lt. Sheehan to training at 2nd Army School of Instruction	
	20th		2nd Lt. W.J. JOHNSTON - formerly a N.C.O in the Batt'n having passed through G.H.Q Cadet School joined the Batt'n	
	22nd		2nd Lt. H.M. BAILLIE promoted LIEUT. - Gazette of this date.	
	23rd		2nd Lt. C.H. SLATER promoted LIEUT. - Gazette of this date.	
	26th		Sunday Training as on 5th.	
	28th		Capt. FAULKNER R.A.M.C. reported for duty to replace Capt. W.W. DICKSON R.M.C.	
	29th		Capt. W.W. DICKSON R.A.M.C. left for HAVRE	

During the month the various companies marched to BAILLEUL in outing arranged by the Div and much appreciated by the men.

C.J. Sheehan Lt. Col.
Comg. 16 R.Ir.Rif.(P)

CONFIDENTIAL.

Army Form C. 2118.

Instructions regarding War Diaries and Intelligence Summaries are contained in F.S. Regs., Part II. and the Staff Manual respectively. Title pages will be prepared in manuscript.

WAR DIARY

INTELLIGENCE SUMMARY.

16TH ROY. IR. RIFS. (PIONEERS).

DECEMBER. 1916. *(Erase heading not required.)*

Place	Date	Hour	Summary of Events and Information	Remarks and references to Appendices
DIVISIONAL AREA.	1st to 31st		Batt. engaged in construction of trench emplacements, trench railways, Russian saps, revetting, training & drainage of communication trenches, screening, hutting, etc.	
	6th		Batt. Hdqrs. moved to NEUVE EGLISE. T.14.d.6.6. No.2 Coy moved to HILLSIDE CAMP. T.14.d.1.6. No.4 Coy moved to HYDE PARK GALLERIES. U.13.d.0.2.	
	19th 28th		Party from ero 3 6° working in SURREY LANE shelled – no casualties. Night party from ero 3 6° in SURREY LANE had one casualty – machine gun fire.	
	29th		Party from ero 36° working in MOB LANE shelled (shrapnel) one casualty.	
			During month Sundays devoted to Infantry training; Lewis Gun training; bombing training, etc.	
			Parties sent during month for courses at 2nd Army School of Snipers and 36th Divl. School of Snipers – good reports received in all cases from Commandants of Schools.	
	21st		Complimentary letter received from G.O.C. 36th Division expressing appreciation of work done by Batt'd during past four months – special mention being made of party who noticed in CALGARY AVENUE and FRONT LINE, under wet & difficult conditions, in one night. letter concludes :– "Officers, N.C.O's and men of the Battalion have worked with a will and with skill and intelligence at all work that has been given them to do and the results are most creditable to the Battalion and worthy of praise."	

Commdg 16/R.I. Rif. (P.)

SECRET.

D.A.G.,
    Base.

        Ref. G.R.O. 1598.

        Herewith please find WAR DIARY of this Battalion for January, 1917.

        Monthly War Diary was formerly rendered to Hd.qrs. 36th (Ulster) Division, but Battalion is now detached from the Division.

                                    Major.

4. 2. 1917   commdg. 16th R. Ir. Rifles (P).

Confidential.

Army Form C. 2118.

WAR DIARY
INTELLIGENCE SUMMARY.
(Erase heading not required.)

Instructions regarding War Diaries and Intelligence Summaries are contained in F.S. Regs., Part II. and the Staff Manual respectively. Title pages will be prepared in manuscript.

JANUARY 1917.

16/ Royal Irish Rifles (P.)

Place	Date	Hour	Summary of Events and Information	Remarks and references to Appendices
	1		Batt. moved to 10th Corps area for work (Railway Instruction) under A.D.L.R.R. 2nd army. Engaged on:—	
	2-31		60 centimetre lines OUDERDOM - KEMMEL; and S.E. BUSSEBOOM. and on Broad gauge line at OUDERDOM. laying steel, packing, ballasting, cranings, sidings, excavating & levelling, ditching, etc. Party working at KEMMEL terminus shelled several times - no casualties. Survey of new 60 centimetre line BUSSEBOOM to DICKIEBUSCH taken up by Lt. C.H. SLATER.	
	19		Lieut. W.D. McKEE. 18th (R) R.I. Rifles joined Battalion.	
	22		2nd/Lt. B. BRADY and D.H. BLACKBURN 20th (R) Batt.R.Ir.Rifles, joined Batt.	
	29		Party in YPRES for bricks suffered two O.R. casualties - one killed, one wounded.	
	31		During month detachment of 3 officers and 100 O.R. engaged with 36th Div. (Provisional) Works Batt^n - casualty, one man killed.	
			Good report received on students who attended 2nd army school of Instruction, January course.	

1.2.1917.

W.J. Allen
Major
Comm^g 16 R.I. Rip (P.)

Confidential.

WAR DIARY
INTELLIGENCE SUMMARY. 16th ROYAL IRISH RIFLES. (PIONEERS).
FEBRUARY, 1917.

Army Form C. 2118.

WO/15

Place	Date	Hour	Summary of Events and Information	Remarks and references to Appendices
	1st to 28th.		Battalion engaged in Railway Construction as follows:— Broad Gauge line at OUDERDOM (sheet 28 N.W. A. 30). 60 Centimetre line :— from N.9 central, sheet 28 S.W. to VIJVERHOEK (H. 29 Central) (sheet 28 N.W.) VIERSTRAAT line; & BUSSEBOOM – OUDERDOM line. and at H. 17. a. (sheet 28. N.W.) S.E. YPRES. Excavation and levelling, laying line, packing & ballasting, crossings, sidings drainage, &c. &c.	
	1.		CAPT. W.B. TANNAHILL, R.A.M.C. joined Battalion on this date as M.O.	
	2.		CAPT. S.B. HAULKENER, R.A.M.C. proceeded to England on being relieved by Capt. TANNAHILL. LT. W.D. McFEE, on being reported to 12th R.I. RIFS. proceeded to join that unit on this date. No 3 Co. at work on VIJVERHOEK line shelled & had to move off — no casualties.	
	12		Draft of 90, O.R. 1/5th LONDON REGIMENT, joined Battalion, also 27 O.R. BEDFORDSHIRE REGT 2nd Lieut d. H.K. FREELAND joined Battalion (commissioned from G.H.Q. Cadet School.) 2nd Lieut H.M. RUTLEDGE, joined Battalion (commissioned from G.H.Q. Cadet School.)	
	20		Draft of 11, O.R. 2/25th LONDON REGT. joined Battalion.	
	24		Draft of 8, O.R. 20th (R) 8th R. IR. RIFS. joined Battalion.	
	26		Infantry training, Lewis gun training & bathing training carried out during month.	

F. Treves
Lieut. Colonel
Commdg. 16th R. Ir. Rif. (P.)
1.3.17.

Confidential.

Army Form C. 2118.

Instructions regarding War Diaries and Intelligence Summaries are contained in F.S. Regs., Part II. and the Staff Manual respectively. Title pages will be prepared in manuscript.

WAR DIARY

INTELLIGENCE SUMMARY.
(Erase heading not required.)

16th ROYAL IRISH RIFLES.(PIONEERS).

MARCH. 1917.

Place	Date	Hour	Summary of Events and Information	Remarks and references to Appendices
	1st to 19th		Battalion engaged on Railway Construction in 10th Corps area as follows:- 60 centimetre gauge lines at:- BUSSEBOOM; BRANDHOEK; KEMMEL branch; VIJVERHOEK branch, etc. and Broad gauge line at OUDERDOM ("B" Supply Siding) laying steel, crossings, sidings, packing and breaching, etc.	
	19th to 23rd		Battalion rejoined 36th Divn	
	23rd to 31st.		Engaged on constructing communication trenches, screening, etc on Divisional front.	
			General. Capt E. SCHERFIELD seriously wounded.	
	12th		2nd Lieut D. PAUL. 18th (R) Batt. Royal Irish Rifles joined for duty.	
	16th		Draft of 12 O.R. (20th (R) Batt. Royal Irish Rifles) joined Battalion.	
	25th		Draft of 11 O.R. (2/25th London Regiment) joined Battalion.	
	26th		No. 570. Rfn. C.V. TAYLOR slightly wounded.	
	26th		During course Infantry training, Lewis gun training, Bombing training, carried out	

1.4.17.

C. Howard Lt.Col.
Comm 16 R.Ir. Rifles (P).

SECRET.

Army Form C. 2118.

Instructions regarding War Diaries and Intelligence Summaries are contained in F.S. Regs., Part II. and the Staff Manual respectively. Title pages will be prepared in manuscript.

WAR DIARY
or
INTELLIGENCE SUMMARY.
(Erase heading not required.)

JM/7

16TH BN ROYAL IRISH RIFLES (PIONEERS)

FOR APRIL 1917.

36th Divisional front (WYTSCHAETE - MESSINES sector)

Place	Date	Hour	Summary of Events and Information	Remarks and references to Appendices
	1st to 30th		Battalion engaged during month on following work:— Construction of communication, reserve and "T" trenches, trench mortar emplacements, screening, dug-outs, railways, &c. NO 1 CO: (less one platoon) working on KERR ST., and KELLY STREET (subsequently renamed THREE K's TRENCH) and later started on new trench (SHEPHERD'S LANE). One platoon NO 1 CO: engaged screening LINDENHOEK LA POLKA ROAD from enemy observation. NO 2 CO: working on GOWER ST., (renamed QUEENS GATE) and a party of same CO: were at work constructing dug-outs on KENNEL HILL, at map Ref. Sheet 28 S.W. N. 25. d. 95. 05. NO. 3 CO: (less one platoon) carried out repair and reclamation of new trench (GEORGE STREET) from PICCADILLY to LONG LANE. Remaining platoon of NO 3 CO: engaged on construction of trench mortar emplacements at different points. NO 4 CO: engaged on construction of new support trench (BOARDMAN	

Secret.

page 2.

Army Form C. 2118.

Instructions regarding War Diaries and Intelligence Summaries are contained in F.S. Regs., Part II. and the Staff Manual respectively. Title pages will be prepared in manuscript.

WAR DIARY
~~or~~
INTELLIGENCE SUMMARY.
(Erase heading not required.)

for April 1917   1st/R. IR. RIFLES (P.)

Place	Date	Hour	Summary of Events and Information	Remarks and references to Appendices
	1st to 30th		TRENCH;) from QUEEN'S GATE to THREE K'S TRENCH, and wiring in front of this trench was also carried out. A small party from Battalion was also engaged on conversion of mere gauge railway to 60 centimetre gauge, from LINDENHOEK – KEMMEL. The above work was greatly retarded during greater part of month owing to very bad weather – snow and rain making work of excavation and drainage very difficult. Good progress however, was made and improved weather conditions towards end of month facilitated erection of work considerably. GENERAL :-	
	14		CASUALTIES. No 26: at work in QUEEN'S GATE heavily shelled. One man killed, one wounded. Trench blown in for about 10 yards, but when shelling ceased repairs were successfully carried out.	
	27		Three men No 46: ___ severely wounded (two by machine gun – one by rifle fire) while out wiring BOARDMAN TRENCH.	

T2134. Wt. W708–776. 500000. 4/15. Sir J. C. & S.

Secret.

page 3.

Army Form C. 2118.

WAR DIARY
INTELLIGENCE SUMMARY.

(Erase heading not required.)

1/6¹ R.IR.RIFS.(F).

for April 1917.

Place	Date	Hour	Summary of Events and Information	Remarks and references to Appendices
	3.		**STRENGTH:-** on 1st April 34 officers. 868 O.R.	
			" 30th " 39 " 866 "	
			REINFORCEMENTS received during month:-	
	5		2ND LIEUT. C. JAGOE and 2ND LIEUT. S. BRYSON, commissioned from 6th O.S. Cadet School.	
			2ND LIEUT. W.S. REA from 18th (R) BATTLN ROYAL IRISH RIFLES.	
	9		7 Other ranks.	
	13		4 do. do.	
	19		4 do. do.	
	20		4 do. do.	
	30		3 do. do.	
	"		CAPT. S.W. KNOX, from sick leave and 2ND LT. W.A. WILSON from 19th (R) Battn. ROYAL IRISH RIFLES.	
			Parties were sent during month to attend courses at:-	
			2nd Army Central School of Instruction.	
			" " Musketry School.	
			" " Cookery School.	
			36th Divn Musketry School.	
			" " Bombing School.	
			" " Physical Training and Bayonet School.	
			TRAINING.	
			During month Infantry Training carried out in Drill, Lewis gun, Bombing, Signalling, etc.	

Secret.

page 4.
WAR DIARY
or
INTELLIGENCE SUMMARY.
(Erase heading not required.)

Army Form C. 2118.

16/ R. IR. RIFS. (P).

30 April 1917

Place	Date	Hour	Summary of Events and Information	Remarks and references to Appendices
	19th		Inoculation against Enteric: enemy return shows that the percentage of all ranks in the Battalion inoculated is 99.8%.	
			Catering: The Instructor in Catering 2nd Army visited Battalion and his report is as follows:- "Very good diet. Puddings almost daily, clean cookhouse, very good stockpot in use. Good messing cook. The messing of this Battalion is above the average, and well supervised."	

1.5.1917.

C.J. Leggard Lt-Colonel
Comm'dg. 16th Batt. ROYAL IRISH RIFLES.
(PIONEERS).

SECRET

Army Form C. 2118.

30/5/3

WAR DIARY

INTELLIGENCE SUMMARY.
(Erase heading not required.)

16TH BN. ROYAL IRISH RIFLES. (PIONEERS)

for MAY. 1917.

Instructions regarding War Diaries and Intelligence Summaries are contained in F.S. Regs., Part II. and the Staff Manual respectively. Title pages will be prepared in manuscript.

Place	Date	Hour	Summary of Events and Information	Remarks and references to Appendices
(WYTSCHAETE - MESSINES sector)	1st to 30th		Battalion engaged during month on following works: Construction of communication trenches, trench mortar emplacements trench railway, screening, dug outs, tracks and bridges for artillery, road repair, etc. NO 1 Cº: working on SHEPPERDS LANE communication trench, Dug outs Brigade Hdqrs. Dug outs, REGENT ST. and screening from enemy observation LINDENHOEK - LA POLKA ROAD, BEAVER HALL - ARCHIE FARM RD. and DRANOUTRE - LINDENHOEK ROAD and several Battery positions. Nº 2 Cº: working on QUEENSGATE and KINGSWAY communication trenches. and a party constructing dugouts on KEMMEL HILL at N.25. N.9.5.05. Sheet 28. S.W. Nº 3 Cº: working on trench mortar emplacements at different points and on repair and extension of GEORGE ST., party from this Cº also at work on Brigade Hdqr. Dugouts at REGENT ST. NO. 4 Cº: engaged on SHEPPERD'S LANE (lower end) FRENCH TRENCH, tracks and bridges for artillery, and repair of road SPY FARM to STORE FARM. A small party from Battalion also engaged on construction of 60 centimetre gauge railway LINDENHOEK & KEMMEL. _____ GENERAL STRENGTH of Battalion at 1st May 1917 39 officers 866 O.R. " " " " 31st " 43 " 956 " 2nd LT. W.A.P. WILLSON, having been posted to 11th BN R. IR. RIFLES. left to join that Battalion.	

36th Division front.

Army Form C. 2118.

page 2.

WAR DIARY

INTELLIGENCE SUMMARY.

(Erase heading not required.)

16th Roy. 2. Rifs. (P.)

Place	Date	Hour	Summary of Events and Information	Remarks and references to Appendices
	May 1917.			
	6.		Reinforcements received during month.	
			CAPT. A.E. FRASER from 18(R) BN. R.IR.RIFS.	
	14		2nd LT. E. CROKER. and 2nd LT. J.C. HODGE, from 18th. R.IR.RIFS.	
	16		62 O.R. from 1/6th LONDON REGIMENT.	
			35 " from 11th Training Reserve Battalion.	
	23		2nd LT. R. KANE from 18th (R) BN. R.IR. RIFS.	
	24		2nd LT. J.H. DOUGAN reposted from 9th BN. R.IR. FUSILIERS.	
			CASUALTIES.	
	1		7208 Sergt. W. FORESTER, wounded.	
			1329 Rfm. R. LEABODY. killed.	
	3		41714 " A.J. BALDWIN. wounded.	
			798 " W.J. LOUDEN. wounded.	
	19		7172 Sgt. A. EDGAR. wounded.	
	30		42084 Rfm. A.C. ABRAHAM. wounded.	
	31		890 Rfm. S. KERR. killed. (gassed)	
			COURSES.	
			Parties were sent during month to attend courses at:-	
			2nd Army School of Instruction.	
			36th Div? Musketry School.	
			" " Lewis Gun "	
			" " Bombing "	
			TRAINING:- During month training carried out in Drill, Lewis Gun,	
			Bombing, Bayonet fighting, Signalling, etc.	

J.L. Stewart
Lieut. Colonel
Comm.dg 16/ R.IR.RIFS. (P.)

1.6.17.

SECRET.
34/5/6.

Army Form C. 2118.

WAR DIARY
INTELLIGENCE SUMMARY
(Erase heading not required.)

Title pages **7th JUNE, 1917** 16TH ROYAL IRISH RIFLES (PIONEERS).

36th Divisional Front.
(WYTSCHAETE – MESSINES) SECTOR
(Sheet 28 S.W.)

Place	Date	Hour	Summary of Events and Information	Remarks and references to Appendices
	1st to 6th		Battalion engaged on construction of Brigade Headquarters Dugouts – REGENT STREET; making tracks from different points behind front line to front line for use of Infantry on "L" day, and also tracks for Artillery; and repairing and cleaning up traffic Road between SPY FARM and STORE FARM.	
	6th.	4 pm.	Battalion Headquarters moved to N.26.c.35.45. KEMMEL HILL, Battle dugout.	
	7th	6.30 am.	6 coys. moved up to position of assembly at N.25.c.5.7. Nos. 1 & 4 coys from hutts in DRANOUTRE, Nos 2 & 6 from BEAVER HALL, & No. 3 6? from LURGAN CAMP.	
	"	8.22 am.	Orders received from C.R.E. 36 Divn. for Nos. 1 & 4 coys to commence work on road clearance and tracks for pack transport respectively. (a) Good progress was made with the road which was eventually put in a serviceable state for wheeled traffic from store farm to a spot beyond SPANBROEKMOLEN MINE CRATER. At commencement of work road was previously non existent, owing to torn-up condition of ground. (b) Two tracks were started from points behind our original front line to BLACK LINE reached by Division, and completed, and were in full use by pack transport from early in the afternoon onwards. Length of right track approximately 2,500 yards (crossing Steenebeek line at N.30.c.1.6.) ending at 0.25.d.1.78.) Length of left track approximately 3,400 yards (crossing Steenebeek line at N.30.a.5.5 and ending at 0.20.c.2.5.) This work entailed considerable labour, as the new covered country by a mass of shell holes. The entire tracks were marked out by white stakes, having tapes being used in difficult places, numbers direction boards were erected and name of track of boards of Broke trenches were put up where crossed by track.	[signature]

2353 Wt. W2544/1454 700,000 5/15 D.D. & L. A.D.S.S./Forms/C. 2118.

SECRET.

Army Form C. 2118.

Instructions regarding War Diaries and Intelligence
Summaries are contained in F.S. Regs., Part II.
and the Staff Manual respectively. Title pages
will be prepared in manuscript.

WAR DIARY

INTELLIGENCE SUMMARY.

(Erase heading not required.)

June 1917.

16th 8th Roy. L. Rifles (Pioneers).

Place	Date	Hour	Summary of Events and Information	Remarks and references to Appendices
	7th	4.33pm	Orders received from C.R.E. for C100. 2 & 3 Coys. to commence work on construction of communication trenches over top of Ridge.	
			(a) OCHRE DRIVE and OCHRE ALLEY C.75. were opened up and made amicable by C/o 2.6: during the night, approximate length 270 yards and 340 yards respectively, average depth 5'.6".	
			(b) OCTOBER AVENUE being completely masked up a new communication trench was dug by C/o 0.3.60. 500 yards to a depth of 6 feet and 200 yards to a depth of 5 feet. Communication	
			The total length of trenches made by these two Companies during the night being over 1300 yards. All these trenches were marked by name boards which had been previously prepared.	
			All ranks work with a will and vigour throughout the operations with the above excellent result.	
		8th	All Coys engaged improving and extending the work commenced on nights of 2 & 3 Coys "stood to" in support of Battalions in the line, during some counterattacks on night 8 & 9.	
		9th	All Coys on same work, C/o H. Coy. in addition engaged making an artillery track from WYTSCHAETE Rd. continued through 0.19.c. Instructions received that Battalion would be engaged under C.E. 9th Corps on construction of trench tramway (DECAUVILLE) from N.29.6.6.2 to 0.25.d.5.5.	
		10th	Work commenced, consisting of making junction (a difficult job) on account of the boggy cut-up condition of ground, laying line, ballasting, ditching etc.	
		11th to 20th	Engaged on same work. Good progress was made, although work was continually interrupted by heavy enemy shelling, particularly at L'ENFER WOOD	

36th Division Front

(WYTSCHAETE — MESSINES SECTOR).

SECRET

Army Form C. 2118.

WAR DIARY
or
INTELLIGENCE SUMMARY.

(Erase heading not required.)

16th Bn. Roy. Irish Rifles (Pioneers)

Instructions regarding War Diaries and Intelligence Summaries are contained in F.S. Regs., Part II. and the Staff Manual respectively. Title pages will be prepared in manuscript.

June 1917.

36th Divisional Front (WYTSCHAETE - MESSINES SECTOR)

Place	Date	Hour	Summary of Events and Information	Remarks and references to Appendices
	21st to 28th		Battalion engaged on construction of communication trenches and repair of roads as follows:- No 1 C.T. between O.15.d.3.2. and O.22.a.1.9 (sheet 28 S.W.) "2 " Repairing and clearing Road from ESTAMINET CROSS ROADS O.20.a.38. to INDE STERKTE CAB. "3 " C.T. BOB TRENCH (between black and MAUVE line) "4 " C.T. BOB TRENCH (between MAUVE LINE and SUPPORT TRENCH) This work had to be carried out at night, and good progress was made, notwithstanding heavy enemy shelling, almost every night.	
	26th		Orders received that Battalion would be transferred to Fifth Army on 30th.	
	29th		REST.	
	30th	4 am.	Battalion moved to new area and on this date were located as follows:- Battalion Headquarters and Coys 3 & 4 Coys at WATOU area Coys 1 & 2 Coys at POPERINGHE.	
			GENERAL:- Strength of Battalion at 1st June 1917 43 Officers. 956 O.R. " " " " 30th " " 1917 44 " 930 " REINFORCEMENTS received during month:- 1. O.R. 16 " 2 " 2nd Lieut. R.M. MARSHALL from 18th (R) R.IR. RIFS. joined Battalion for duty. 5. O.R. 15 " 17 " 24 " 27 "	

2353 Wt. W2544/1454 700,000 5/15 D.D.&L. A.D.S.S./Forms/C. 2118.

'SECRET'

Army Form C. 2118.

Instructions regarding War Diaries and Intelligence Summaries are contained in F. S. Regs., Part II. and the Staff Manual respectively. Title pages will be prepared in manuscript.

WAR DIARY
or
INTELLIGENCE SUMMARY.
16th Royal Irish Rifles (Pioneers)

(Erase heading not required.)

June 1917.

Place	Date	Hour	Summary of Events and Information	Remarks and references to Appendices
			CASUALTIES.	
			killed. wounded. wounded & gassed. shellshock.	
	7th		1 3	
	15th		1 1	
	18th		5 7	
	19th		4 6	
	22nd		. 2	
	24th		. 1	
	25th		. 1 1	
	26th		. . 1 1	
	27th		1 1	
			9 23 1 1	
			Horses:- Gas attended and slung to central reserve of evacuation during month & an excellent report received from school.	

W. Allen
Major
Commanding 16th R.I.R. Rifles C.P.S.

SECRET.

Instructions regarding War Diaries and Intelligence Summaries are contained in F. S. Regs., Part II. and the Staff Manual respectively. Title pages will be prepared in manuscript.

Army Form C. 2118.

WAR DIARY
or
INTELLIGENCE SUMMARY.
(Erase heading not required.)

16th ROYAL IRISH RIFLES (PIONEERS)

July. 1917.

Place	Date	Hour	Summary of Events and Information	Remarks and references to Appendices
YPRES SECTOR. BACK AREA.	1.		LOCATION of Battalion: Headquarters and Nos. 3 & 4 Coys. at WATOU. Nos. 1 and 2 Coys. at POPERINGHE.	
	2.		No.1 Coy. moved to NORMHOUDT.	
	3.		No.2 Coy. moved to WINNEZEELE.	
	4.		No.1 Coy. moved to BOLLEZEELE.	
	5 to 11		Rest.	
			Coys. commenced sinking wells, to augment water supply, in the areas in which they were located.	
			Engaged on same work.	
			No. 4 Coy. moved to E.11.b.8.5. Sheet 27 for training in rapid construction of Light Railways.	
			No.3 Coy. moved to L.7.d.1.3, Sheet 27 to be nearer work.	
	12		Nos. 1, 2 & 3 Coys. engaged on wells.	
	13		No.1 Coy. moved to C. 30. b. 2.2. Sheet 27.	
	14 15 to 20		Coys. 1, 2 & 3 Coys. on wells.	
	21		Battalion Headquarters, Nos. 1, 2 & 3 Coys. moved to camp outside POPERINGHE at G. 13. b. 9.5 sheet 28.	
FORWARD AREA.	22. 23		Battalion Infantry training.	
			"B" Party of No.3 Coy. started work on repair of road from HELLFIRE CORNER to DRAGOON FARM (1.10.c.9.2 to I.14.d.0.2 Sheet 28. N.W.) Owing to heavy shelling by enemy with Gas shells, work was slow and conditions became so difficult that party had to knock off at 12.30 a.m. 2nd Lieut. J. BRYSON and No. 4/1989 RFN. C. ROPER admitted to hospital, gassed.	
	24.		"B" Party of No. 2 Coy. repairing Road HELLFIRE CORNER - DRAGOON FARM. Good progress was made, notwithstanding heavy shelling (Gas shells) until 1.30 a.m. 25th. when conditions became very bad and working party had to withdraw.	
			"A" Party of No.1 Coy. engaged cleaning branch line from I.15. a. o. to I. 14. b. 45. Sheet 28 N.W. (from MOFFAT to RAILWAY) S.E. of YPRES). Work could only be done	

2353 Wt. W2544/1454 700,000 5/15 D. D. & L. A.D.S.S./Forms/C. 2118.

SECRET.

Army Form C. 2118.

WAR DIARY
or
INTELLIGENCE SUMMARY.
(Erase heading not required.)

Instructions regarding War Diaries and Intelligence Summaries are contained in F. S. Regs., Part II. and the Staff Manual respectively. Title pages will be prepared in manuscript.

16th ROYAL IRISH RIFLES. (PIONEERS).

July. 1917

Place	Date	Hour	Summary of Events and Information	Remarks and references to Appendices
YPRES SECTOR	24		at work intervals owing to enemy gas shelling.	
	25		Party from C/O 3 by. gunning to assist HELLFIRE CORNER ROAD - was considerably retarded owing to gas shelling, and party had to return off about 3 am. - one man wounded.	
	"		Party from C/O 1 by. continued work on CHANNEL and got it completed, notwithstanding heavy shellfire - casualties, one officer (2nd Lieut C.B. JAGOE) and 5. O.R. killed and 3 O.R. wounded.	
	26 30		Bys. engaged in Infantry training etc.	
	31		Third battle of YPRES.	
		5.30 a.m.	Battalion working under C.E. 19th Corps. allotted task of clearing and repairing Road from German front line at C.23.c.8.2., sheet 28 N.W. to BOSSART FARM (C.23. b.3.0. the object being to make road fit as rapidly as possible to allow heavy artillery into advanced positions. C/O 1.by. moved up to commence work on road. This was found to be non-existent the alignment only being visible owing to the unevenly, the enemy shelling was rather not commenced until 12 noon. At 3.30 pm. road had been levelled and cleared to take limber over a distance of 350 yards from German front line towards BOSSART FARM.	
		3.30 pm.	From this hour until 5.30 pm. the road was subjected to very heavy shellfire rendering work impossible. shelling continued throughout the night, and rain having come in, the road soon developed into a quagmire. Under such adverse conditions, C/O 3 & C/O 2 Bys (who relieved C/O 1 by. at 5.30 pm.) concentrated on getting up material as close as possible to cover the scene of the work.	Casualties

$353 Wt. W3544/1454 700,000 5/15 D. D. & L. A.D.S.S./Forms/C. 2118.

SECRET.

Army Form C. 2118.

WAR DIARY
or
INTELLIGENCE SUMMARY.
(Erase heading not required.)

16th ROYAL IRISH RIFLES (PIONEERS)

Instructions regarding War Diaries and Intelligence Summaries are contained in F. S. Regs., Part II. and the Staff Manual respectively. Title pages will be prepared in manuscript.

Place	Date	Hour	Summary of Events and Information	Remarks and references to Appendices
YPRES SECTOR	31		Casualties sustained were as follows:- C/o L.O. 3 O.R. killed; 1 Officer. (Lt. H.H.R. DOLLING) and 5. O.R. wounded = 6. " 3 " 5. O.R. " 2 officers. (2/Lt. L.N. ROSS.D and 6. O.R. wounded = 8 " 8 " " 3 " " " " " " = 14 C/o 36: 1 O.R. missing. GENERAL:- Strength of Battalion at 12 noon 1st July 1917. 44 officers. 930. O.R. " " " " " 31st " " 41 " 913 " Reinforcements received during month. 7	Hon. Lieut. & Qr.mr. J.W. GORDON reported for duty. 8	2 O.R. arrived from Base. 19	6 " " " " CASUALTIES during month:- 			KILLED	WOUNDED	MISSING 			Offrs. O.R.	Offrs. O.R.	Offrs. O.R. 6	C/o 44579 Rfn. W.H. WILKINSON, accidentally drowned. — 1 — 1 — — 23	— 5 1 4 — — 26	— 8 — 11 — 1 31	— 13 1 16 — 1 (signed) O.J. Bowen (?) Lt. Colonel. Commanding Roy. Ir. Rif. (P)

1st August 1917.

Army Form C. 2118.

8/34.

Instructions regarding War Diaries and Intelligence Summaries are contained in F.S. Regs., Part II. and the Staff Manual respectively. Title pages will be prepared in manuscript.

WAR DIARY
INTELLIGENCE SUMMARY.
(Erase heading not required.)

16th ROYAL IRISH RIFLES (PIONEERS)

AUGUST 1917.

Place	Date	Hour	Summary of Events and Information	Remarks and references to Appendices
YPRES FRONT	1st to 4th		Battalion (less NO4 Coy) on light railways located at H.11. & 9.1. 28. N.W. Battalion (less No 4 Coy) departed for light Railway Construction, continued work on repair of WIELTJE - SPREE FM ROAD. This proved very difficult work owing to bad weather conditions and heavy enemy shelling. The portion of Road Battalion engaged on was from Oblegman's Junction at C.23.C.3.2. to C.23.d.3.9. Sheet 28.N.W. 2. ED.6.A. ST. JULIEN. Continuous heavy rain quickly reduced the site of the road to a quagmire, rendering progress very slow. Shovel work carried out under C.E. 19th Corps. Battalion rejoined 36th Divn to camp at H.10.C.2.3. - 28.N.W. (S.E. VLAMERTINGHE).	
	5/6th		Nos 1 and 2 Coys started work on draining, repairing and laying trenchboards in CARNATION TRENCH and CAPTAIN AVENUE (EAST of WIELTJE) No 3 Coy engaged in repair of WIELTJE - SPREE FARM ROAD commencing at C.23.d.2.8 Sheet 28.N.W. and working N.E.	
	6/7th to 13/14th		Engaged on same work. Good progress was made despite very bad weather conditions and heavy enemy shelling.	
	14/15th		Nos. 1, 2 & 3 Coys engaged prolonging Nos. 4, 5 & 6 tracks for pack transport etc., to front line preparatory to operations on 16th.	
	15th		Advanced 83? Hdqs. established at I.1.d.8.1. (SH.28.N.W.)	
	16th		Battle (see narrative attached)	
	17th		Companies moved back to camp at H.10.C.2.3. (28.N.W.)	

2333 Wt W2544/1454 700,000 5/15 D.D.&L. A.D.S.S./Forms/C. 2118.

Army Form C. 2118.

WAR DIARY
INTELLIGENCE SUMMARY.

16th ROYAL IRISH RIFLES (PIONEERS).

AUGUST. 1917.

Instructions regarding War Diaries and Intelligence Summaries are contained in F. S. Regs., Part II. and the Staff Manual respectively. Title pages will be prepared in manuscript.

(Erase heading not required.)

Place	Date	Hour	Summary of Events and Information	Remarks and references to Appendices
YPRES FRONT	18th to 21st		Nos. 1, 2 & 3 6 Coys. engaged in repair of WIELTJE - SPREE FARM ROAD, commencing at C.23.d.3.9. & working N.E., and completing road clearance and repair to C.23.b.45.05 (sheet 28.N.W.)	
	21st.		Received instructions from 36th Division that the Battalion would proceed with Division on 23rd August to the SOMME in preparation for training. Telegram from 19th Corps that the Battalion (including No. 4 & 16th Coys) moved proceed on 22nd inst. to join 36th Division in WINNIZEELE No 2 area. No. 4 Coy. rejoined Battalion. Battalion proceeded by bus to C.4.a. sheet 27 (Belgium & France) WINNIZEELE No 2 area.	
	22nd.		Instructions received through 36th Division, from 19th Corps, that Battalion would be left behind when Division proceeded to 2nd army area.	
	23rd.		At J.4.w. sheet 27. Instructions received from 36th Division that Battalion would come on & come first to camp at A.20.d.3.2. sheet 28.N.W.	
	24th 25th		At J.4.a. sheet 27	
	26th		Battalion H. Qrs. and Nos. 3 & 4 Coys. moved to camp at A.28.d.5.2. sh.28.N.W. and Nos. 1 & 2 Coys. to H.4.C.3.7. sh.28.N.W. and came under C.E.18th Corps for work.	
	27th		Instructions received that Battalion H.Q. and 2 Coys. would move to CANAL BANK dugouts (N. of YPRES.) C.25.d.1.8. sh.28.N.W. on 29th August.	
	28th		No.16 Coy. engaged in repair & upkeep of CUFFS RD. from C.22.C.6.3.50 to C.22.C.7.1.(sh.28.N.W.) No. 20 Coy. engaged in repair & upkeep of ADMIRAL RD. from C.22.C.6.3.50 to C.22.d.2.0. (sh.28.N.W.)	

YPRES FRONT

Army Form C. 2118.

WAR DIARY
or
INTELLIGENCE SUMMARY.
(Erase heading not required.)

16th ROYAL IRISH RIFLES (PIONEERS).

AUGUST 1917.

Place	Date	Hour	Summary of Events and Information	Remarks and references to Appendices
YPRES FRONT (ST JULIEN SECTOR)	29th		Bn. H.Q. Nos. 3 & 4 Coys & ½ No. 1 Coy. moved to CANAL BANK, YPRES, and ½ No. 1 Coy. to shelters at ENGLISH FARM. C. 27. b. 5. 3. Sheet 28. N.W. Transport located at H. 3. b. 2. 7.	
	30/31st		No. 1 Coy. engaged on repair of WIELTJE – ST. JULIEN RD. from C. 23. a. 4. 2. to TRIANGLE FARM. No. 2 Coy. on improvements to REIGERSBURG CAMP in H. 6. a. Sheet 28. N.W. No. 3 Coy. on repair & prolongation of trench board tracks from ADMIRALS RD. (C. 22. a. 5. 0 – 28. N.W.) past MOUSE TRAP FM., JULIET FARM to the STEENBEEK. No. 4 Coy. on repair and prolongation of trench board tracks from ADMIRALS ROAD (C. 22. a. 1. 4) past HAMPSHIRE FARM, ALBERTA FARM, past HAMPSHIRE FARM, ALBERTA FARM, thence towards TRIANGLE FARM. and repair and prolongation of mule tracks running from ADMIRALS ROAD (C. 22. a. 1. 3) forward to ALBERTA. This work was under C.R.E. 55th Division.	
	1st to 21st		Orders received from C.R.E. 55th Division that battalion would be transferred to 19th Corps and at 9pm for work with 42nd Division. During this period No. 1 & 2 were engaged with new services rly. coy. on construction of light railways, WEST, NORTH and EAST of YPRES.	

Army Form C. 2118.

16th ROYAL IRISH RIFLES (P.J.)

WAR DIARY
INTELLIGENCE SUMMARY.
(Erase heading not required.)

August 1917.

Instructions regarding War Diaries and Intelligence Summaries are contained in F.S. Regs., Part II. and the Staff Manual respectively. Title pages will be prepared in manuscript.

Place	Date	Hour	Summary of Events and Information	Remarks and references to Appendices
			General:-	
			Strength of Battalion at 12 noon 31st July, 1917. 41 Offrs. 913. O.R.	
			" " " " " 31st August 1917 39 " 845 O.R.	
			Reinforcements received during month.	
	22		2nd Lt. A.N.G. S'KELLY and 2nd Lt. E.W. LOGAN, joined for duty from 20(R)Bt R.IR.RIFS.	
			Draft of 26. O.R. arrived.	
	27		Draft of 26 O.R. arrived under 36th Divn for Battalion.	
			Casualties during month:-	
			Killed. Died of Wounds. Missing. Wounded. Shellshock.	
			O. O.R. O. O.R. O. O.R. O. O.R. O. O.R.	
1			2 1 5	
2			1 2	
3			3 3	
5			2	
6			1 1	
7			9	
8			9	
9			2 1	
11			2	
12			3 1 12	(2/Lt. H.H. RUTLEDGE)
13			2	(2/Lt. D.H. BLACKBURN)
14			1 1	
16			1	
17				
18			1	
19				
22			2	
27			2	
30				
			8 4 1 62. 1	

[signature] J. Furness
Lt. Colonel
Commdg. 16/R.IR. RIFS(P.I)

1.9.17.

NARRATIVE

of part taken by 16th BN. ROY.IR.RIFS.(P).
(less one Coy.) during OPERATIONS on the
16th. August, 1917.

My Battalion, less one Coy., moved into Billets in YPRES on night of 15th/16th August, 1917, and my Advanced Hdqrs. was also established in a Dug-out on CANAL BANK at I. 1. b. 8.1. Sheet 28. N.W.

My original Orders from C.R.E., were :-

    1 Coy. to work on No. 4 Track.
    1 " to work on No. 5 "
    1 " to work on No. 6 "

to continue these from the present Front line up to the new positions, also a small party of 1 Officer and 12 men to clear WIELTJE - GRAVENSTAFEL RD. where it crossed the Black Line.

These Orders were subsequently cancelled and fresh orders were received from C.R.E. at about 8.30 p.m. on night 15/16th August, as follows:-

    WIELTJE - GRAVENSTAFEL RD. 2 Coys.
    No. 6 Track. ½ Coy.
    No. 4 Track. ½ Coy.

A turning place to be made on Road where it crosses HANEBEEK for Ambulances, until crater was made passable. Materials to be drawn from revetments in CARNATION TRENCH, etc.

No. 5 Track to be linked into Road near BANK FARM.

Orders were received from C.R.E. about 10 p.m. for Coys to move up from billets in YPRES without further orders on morning on 16th. so as to commence work as soon after Zero as possible. All parties moved up from billets before 4 a.m. and commenced work on their allotted tasks very soon after the attack was launched, but did not manage to do very much work before things became impossible by the enemy's barrage and machine-gun fire and the eventual retirement of the attacking troops back to the original front line.

The party of 1 Officer and 12 men managed to clear the road across the black line as ordered and then rejoined their Coy.

The half Coy. on No. 4 Track under Lieut. Sheehan got the Black Line partially filled in to take track over, and ran tape and stakes out as far as Hill 35, but then had to assemble to assist the Infantry in their retirement.

The half Coy. on No. 6 Track finished off the Track up to the Black Line and then had to knock off owing to the barrage and machine-gun fire. Captain Chase, who was in charge, then ordered the half Coy. back to billets in YPRES as he saw there was nothing to be done, but remained himself with another Officer to see if conditions would improve.

1.

Army Form C. 2118.

WAR DIARY
INTELLIGENCE SUMMARY.

(Erase heading not required.)

16th BN ROYAL IRISH RIFLES (PIONEERS).

September, 1917.

Place	Date	Hour	Summary of Events and Information	Remarks and references to Appendices
YPRES SECTOR	1		Battalion moved to camp at H.7. c.5.3, 28.N.W (S. of BRANDHOEK)	
	2		Received instructions from C.R.E. 42nd Division that two coys would move on 3rd inst. to Infantry Barracks, YPRES & construct dug.outs there to be used as billets.	
	3		Nos. 2 & 4 Coys moved to Infantry Barracks, YPRES, and were employed on construction of dug.outs. No.1 Coy employed on road construction at Ammunition Dump, MOAT FM. (H.17.c.8.4, 28.N.W.) No.3 Coy employed on road construction at H.7.d.3.8. and at VANCOUVER DUMP, H.8.d.7.3, both 28.N.W.	
	4		Same work. No. 4 Coy. commenced construction of trench Railway from I.10.a.9.1 through I.11.b.0.5, along old railway to RIFLEWAY WOOD (Ref. ZILLEBEKE sheet 28.N.W. & N.E.S.(parts)) Work delayed owing to shelling. Billets in YPRES came under heavy gas shelling.	
	5		No. 4 Coy. on railway construction. No. 2 Coy commenced work on construction of strong points on WESTHOEK RIDGE J.1.a.5.2.; J.1.c.6.7. and J.1.c.8.3. (sheet: ZILLEBEKE) Nos. 1 & 3 Coys on road construction.	
	6		Coys. on work as above.	
	7		Orders received from 12th Infantry Brigade that in case of hostile attack at night, the two coys engaged in constructing strong points at WESTHOEK RIDGE would man same and for tactical purposes be under Battalion commander at KIT and KAT.	
	8		Coys engaged in usual work. Work of 2 & 4 Coys greatly delayed owing to heavy shelling.	
	9			
	10			

Army Form C. 2118.

WAR DIARY
INTELLIGENCE SUMMARY.
(Erase heading not required.)

September 1917

16th R. IR. RIFS. (P.)

Place	Date	Hour	Summary of Events and Information	Remarks and references to Appendices
YPRES SECTOR.	11		No 1 Coy. relieved No 2 Coy. & took over construction of strong points.	
			" 3 " " 4 " " " " " " trench Railway	
	12 13		Nos. 1 & 4 Coys on Road construction	
	14		Coys on same work.	
	15		No 1 Coy. finished work on strong points & started digging trench at J. 2. a. 0. 5 (ZILLEBEKE sheet)	
	16		All Coys on same work. No. 1 Coy. also had a party screening YPRES—MENIN R.R.	
	17		Orders received from C.R.E. 42 nd Division that Coys 1 & 3 Coys then billeted in YPRES would rejoin Battalion in camp at J. 7. c. 5. 3. 25 N.W. on 18th inst.	
	18		Nos. 1 & 3 Coys. moved back to camp	
	19		Orders received from 5th Bde G. to be in readiness to move on 20th inst to 3rd Army area, detailed orders to be issued later. Orders received from 5th Bde G. that 85" would entrain at VLAMERTINGHE for YPRES on 20 th inst. Transport at 6 a.m.; Remainder at 10.30 a.m.	
	20		Battalion entrained as per orders & left VLAMERTINGHE at 12.15 p.m.	
	21		Battalion arrived at YPRES, SOMME at 6 a.m. & marched to billets in camp N. of BERTINCOURT.	
	22 & 27		Infantry training	
HAVRINCOURT FRONT (CONT.)	28 29 30		Battalion engaged wiring barbed wire entanglements — in double apron belts between K. 19. C. 4. 8 and K. 20. c. 1. 1 (sheet 57 c. FRANCE) a distance of 1800 yards. This work was completed in two nights in all 4400 yards of wire. Commenced construction of a "SWITCH" trench from K. 19. c. 2.5 to K. 26. c. 1. 9. sheet 57 c. F. FRANCE) a distance of 1500 yards	

Army Form C. 2118.

WAR DIARY
or
INTELLIGENCE SUMMARY.
(Erase heading not required.)

16th R: IR: RIFS. (P.)

Title pages September 1917.

Place	Date	Hour	Summary of Events and Information	Remarks and references to Appendices
			GENERAL :- Strength of Battalion at 12 noon 31st August 1917. Offrs 39. O.R. 845	
			" " " " " " " 30th Septr 1917. " 38. " 790	
			Reinforcements received during month :-	
	4		11 O.R. draft joined Bn from Base.	
	9		7 " " " " " "	
	12		1st Lt J.E. McCLELLAND joined Battalion.	
	15		10 O.R. draft joined Battalion.	
	23		1 O.R. transferred to Battalion from 14th R.IR. RIFS.	
			15 " " draft taken on strength of Battalion.	
	26		LT. C.W. HINDS taken on strength of Bn.	
			Casualties during month :-	
			K. W. (GASSED) W.	
			O. O.R. O. O.R. O. O.R.	
	6		- - - 2. - 27.	
	6		- - - 2. - -	
	8		1 - x1. 7 1 6 ✗ CAPT. W.R. WHITE.	
	10		- - - 5. - 5	
	11		- - - - - -	
	13		- - x1. 4 - 5 ✗ 2nd Lt. FREELAND (slightly, at duty)	
	17		- - - 1. - -	
			1 - 2. 21. 1 44	
	14		2nd Lt. R.M. MARSHALL to hospital (sick)	
	18		Capt. C.A. SLATER & 2nd Lt. J.C. HODGE to hospital (sick)	
	22		2/Lt. R. KANE " " " "	
	24		Lieut. A. GREEN " " " "	

M. Allen Major
Commdg 16th R. IR RIFS (P)
1.10.1917.

Army Form C. 2118.

VL 23

Scout C/58

16th Bⁿ Rgt. 2. Rfp. (P.)

Instructions regarding War Diaries and Intelligence Summaries are contained in F.S. Regs., Part II. and the Staff Manual respectively. Title pages will be prepared in manuscript.

WAR DIARY
or
INTELLIGENCE SUMMARY.
(Erase heading not required.)

October 1917.

Place	Date	Hour	Summary of Events and Information	Remarks and references to Appendices
	1st.		Battalion located at BERTINCOURT, E. of BAPAUME, SOMME. All coys. continued work on digging SWITCH LINE from K.19.c.25 to K.26.c.1.9. (Reference MOEUVRES E.D. 2.C. special sheet, parts of 57 c.N.W. & N.E.) A work party was engaged on drainage in VELU WOOD. Work on SWITCH LINE continued.	
	2.3.			
	4.		Companies engaged on "RAY" wiring of SWITCH LINE, and on widening & deepening this line. Enemy shelling delayed this work. — 6 men wounded.	
	5.		"Ray" wiring continued and sandbagging of fire bays & parapets put in hand. 9 "flying traverses" were also commenced.	
	6.		"Ray" wiring completed. Work continued on parapets & fire bays. Revetting of fire steps commenced, also construction of drains & sump pits.	
	7.8.		Above work continued. do.	
			Orders received from 36th Divn. G.(6.x.274) that one platoon would move to LECHELLE area and instructions for work on hutting in corps Reserve area. Work to start on 10th inst.	
	9.		Drainage etc. of SWITCH LINE continued. 1 platoon of Coy 2 Coy. moved to LECHELLE for work on hutting under Adjutant E. CROKER. Transport moved to YTRES.	
			Drainage etc. of SWITCH LINE continued.	
	10.		do. Coy 3 Coy. moved to ROYALCOURT.	
	11.		" 4 " moved to METZ.	
	12.		Drainage in VELU WOOD completed. Work on SWITCH LINE. Nos. 1 & 2 Coys. continued work on SWITCH LINE. Nos. 3 & 4 Coys. at work erecting camps & quarters.	

HAVRINCOURT FRONT
SOMME.

Army Form C. 2118.

WAR DIARY
INTELLIGENCE SUMMARY.
(Erase heading not required.)

October 1917.   16th Bn Roy. L. Rif. (P.)

Place	Date	Hour	Summary of Events and Information	Remarks and references to Appendices
HAVRINCOURT FRONT SOMME	13		No 1 Coy. engaged in drainage & grading of SWITCH LINE. No 2 – small party engaged in enlarging "Irish" drain over HERMIES-BERTINCOURT RD. at "Stag Stop" remainder (less platoon in hutting) preparing winter quarters at BERTINCOURT.	
	14		Nos. 1 & 2 Coys. draining & grading SWITCH LINE. Nos 3 & 4 Coys. working on winter quarters.	
	15		Nos. 1 & 2 Coys. on same work. No. 3 Coy. started work on section of double apron wiring INTERMEDIATE LINE through HAVRINCOURT LINE from Q.8.b.7.5. to K.31.a.5.8. (sheet BEAUCHAMP) No. 4 Coy. started work same as No 3 Coy. from Q.8.b.7.5. to Q.8.d.5.5.	
	16		All Coys. on same work. No 2 Coy. started work in repair HERMIES-BERTINCOURT ROAD.	
	17 to 21		All Coys. on same work.	
	22 23		All Coys. engaged on digging new line from K.20.d.12.06 to K.26.a.35.70 to K.26.a.53.40. Sheet HERMIES. 6a.4a. 1/10,000.	
	23 24 25		Above work continued and finished work on new line by evo. 1 & 2 Coys. Nos. 3 & 4 Coys. on mining in HAVRINCOURT WOOD. No 4 Coy. continued work on Switch line. (LURGAN SWITCH) " 2. " " " Irish drain and Road repair. No. 3 & 4 Coys. continued wiring in HAVRINCOURT WOOD.	
	26 to 31st		All Coys. on same work.	

Army Form C. 2118.

WAR DIARY

INTELLIGENCE SUMMARY.

(Erase heading not required.)

October 1917.   16th Bn. Royal Irish Rifles (Pioneers)

Place	Date	Hour	Summary of Events and Information	Remarks and references to Appendices
			General. Strength of Battalion on 1st October 1917. Offrs. 39 O.R. 795 " " " 31st October 1917. " 41 " 789	
	1		**Reinforcements received during month:-** 53 O.R. Lt. J.A.W. McCrucian joined for duty. 2nd Lieuts. R.J. McNEICE, 2nd Lieut. R. THOMPSON, 2nd Lieut. E.V. BRIGGS, 2nd Lieut. W.H. ROBINSON, 2nd Lieut. H.C. GILMORE, 2nd Lieut. T. BROWN, joined for duty from 15th(R)8th R.IR. RIFS. (P)	
	25			
			Casualties during month.	
			Killed. Wounded. Died of wounds.	
	4		- 5 O.R. -	
	11		- - 1 O.R.	
	17		1 O.R. - -	
	28		- 1 -	
			1. 6. 1.	
	27		CAPT. C.D. CHASE proceeded to 2nd Army HQrs. for employment as a "P.B" officer. (Authority A.G's. A/13/238 dated 16.10.17).	
	8		2/Lt. J.R. KANE, invalided to England.	
	20		" J.C. HODGE " " "	
	21		" R.M. MARSHALL " " "	

Army Form C. 2118.

WAR DIARY
INTELLIGENCE SUMMARY.

(Erase heading not required.)

October 1917.   16th Bn. Roy. Ir. Rifles. (P).

Place	Date	Hour	Summary of Events and Information	Remarks and references to Appendices
			During the month parties were sent to courses at:- IV th Corps Lewis Gun & Bombing school. do. Infantry school. 36th Division Gas school. Veterinary Hospital ABBEVILLE.	
	1.11.1917		*[signature]* Lieut. Colonel. Commanding 16th R. IR. RIFLES (P.)	

WAR DIARY

INTELLIGENCE SUMMARY.

NOVEMBER 1917.

16th Bn. ROYAL IRISH RIFLES (Pioneers)

Place: HAVRINCOURT FRONT
REF. SHEET. 57° FRANCE. S.E. & N.E.

Date	Hour	Summary of Events and Information	Remarks and references to Appendices
1		No.1 Coy. grading and draining "LURGAN SWITCH". No.2 " Completed "Irish Drain" and continued on repair of road at SLAG HEAP. " 3 " on repair of Road from METZ to PLACE MORTEMART (HAVRINCOURT WOOD) " 4 " on repair of main METZ - TRESCAULT ROAD.	
2		All Coys. continued same work.	
3		do	
4 & 5		No.2 Coy. also started on repair of road from J.34.d.30.50 towards HERMIES. This Coy also had a party on repair of hindered diversion round crater. BERTINCOURT-HERMIES ROAD (at P.3a.85.30.)	
6		All coys. on same work. Three platoons No.1 Coy. started on repair of Road from SLAG HEAP to WINDY CORNER (HERMIES). 1 platoon remained at work on LURGAN SWITCH. Other coys. on usual work.	
7		All No.2 Coy. concentrated on hindered diversion round crater. BERTINCOURT-HERMIES ROAD. Remaining Coys. on usual work.	
8 to 15		All coys. on same work.	
16		Nos. 1, 2 & 3 Coys. moved to billets in VELU WOOD, near crateau. B = Oys. moved to I.29.d.7.3 (Sheet 57° FRANCE)	
17		Nos. 1, 2 & 3 coys. at work on construction of dugouts at HERMIES, and on repair from SLAG HEAP to WINDY CORNER. No. 2 Coy. continued work on crater diversion.	
18		No. 4 Coy. moved from METZ to HAVRINCOURT WOOD (G.14.C.5.9.)	
19		Coys. 1, 2 & 3 coys. moved to tented camp, near Beet Root Factory, METZ. G = Coy moved to HAVRINCOURT WOOD (G.15.d.0.4.)	

Secret.

Army Form C. 2118.

Instructions regarding War Diaries and Intelligence Summaries are contained in F.S. Regs., Part II. and the Staff Manual respectively. Title pages will be prepared in manuscript.

WAR DIARY or INTELLIGENCE SUMMARY.
(Erase heading not required.)

16 m.o. 2nd R. IR. RIFS. (P.)

Place	Date	Hour	Summary of Events and Information	Remarks and references to Appendices
	NOVEMBER 1917		BATTLE ON CAMBRAI FRONT.	
	20		The following work was allotted to Battalion in conjunction with Divisional R.E:- (a) Preparation of a 20' track from 8.10.a.H.H to RIBECOURT, for cavalry. (b) Repair and improve road from 9.10.a.44 to RIBECOURT, to make it passable for lorries. The work on above to be done by Battalion was distributed as follows:- No.1 COY. (under CAPT. H.L. DICKSON) to do diversion round crater in K.36.C.05.10. and road repair on diversion up to, but exclusive of, crater at K.36.C.Y.Y. and trench crossing near crater at K.36.C.05.10. No.2 COY. (under CAPT. H.J. SHEEHAN) to do diversion round crater at K.36.C.Y.Y. and diversions on road repair up to, but exclusive of, trench crossing at K.36.C.2.3. and intermediate crossings. No.3 COY. (under CAPT. W.4. MADDEN) and No.4 COY. (under CAPT. A.D. FRASER) to do clearance or diversion of road from K.36.C.2.3. to RIBECOURT, exclusive of trench crossings.	
		a.m. 7.0.	All coys. moved to assembly positions in HAVRINCOURT WOOD (8.14.a DC)	
		7.15.	O.C. Battalion left for scene of work to examine same.	
		9.50	Nos. 1 & 2 coys. moved forward and commenced work allotted to them.	
			Nos. 3 & 4 coys. moved forward to rear of TRESCAULT in readiness to commence work.	
		10.30	Nos. 3 & 4 coys. commenced work allotted to them. Track to allow cavalry through completed in time allotted (2 hours) and road repair etc. started on. This work went on steadily enough out the day and good progress made. Conditions favourable, save for occasional shelling. 2nd Lieutenant M.G. Fine from FLESQUIERES direction. CASUALTIES:- 2.O.R. wounded (one of whom subsequently died)	

Secret.

WAR DIARY

INTELLIGENCE SUMMARY
(Erase heading not required.)

November 1917.   16th ROY. IR. RIFS. (P.)

Army Form C. 2118.

Instructions regarding War Diaries and Intelligence Summaries are contained in F.S. Regs., Part II. and the Staff Manual respectively. Title pages will be prepared in manuscript.

Place	Date	Hour	Summary of Events and Information	Remarks and references to Appendices
RIBECOURT SECTOR	21		Above work continued, and although rain made conditions difficult good progress was made.	
	22		Work continued until 12 noon, when road passed fit for lorry traffic and being used by lorries. Orders received from C.R.E. 36th Divn. that Battalion would move to camp in vicinity of HERMIES at U.30.d. on 23rd inst. 1, 2 & 3 Coys. moved back to old camp at METZ. No. 4 Coy. to works previously occupied in HAVRINCOURT WOOD.	
	23	7.a.m.	Battalion moved to camp at J.30.d. (N. of Cemetery) Orders received from R.E. that two Coys. would be engaged on road repair from :- DEMICOURT up to BAPAUME - CAMBRAI x road and two Coys. on similar work on HERMIES - GRAINCOURT RD from K.19.C.H.9. to CHINESE WALL (K.14.C.3.9. approximately).	
		6.p.m.	Telegram received from C.R.E. for two Coys. to be held in readiness to proceed at 6.30 a.m. 24th inst. on special work (This work to consist of the construction of causeways over canal at K.9.C.2.H. and K.9. central (approximately) to take Yankee tanks.)	
HOEUVRES SECTOR	24.		No.1 Coy. commenced repair of DEMICOURT RD. up to BAPAUME - CAMBRAI cross roads. - Work interrupted on several occasions owing to enemy shellfire. No.3 Coy. commenced repair of Road :- HERMIES - GRAINCOURT. No.2 Coy. commenced and completed causeway over canal at K.9. central. No.4 " commenced and completed causeway over canal at K.9.C.2.H.	

Secret.

Army Form C. 2118.

Instructions regarding War Diaries and Intelligence Summaries are contained in F. S. Regs., Part II. and the Staff Manual respectively. Title pages will be prepared in manuscript.

WAR DIARY
INTELLIGENCE SUMMARY.
(Erase heading not required.)

1 Bn. ROY. IR. RIFS. (P.)

November 1917.

Place	Date	Hour	Summary of Events and Information	Remarks and references to Appendices
	25		Nos. 1 & 2 Coys. continued repair of DEMICOURT R.D. forward. Nos. 3 & 4 Coys. " " " HERMIES - GRAINCOURT R.D.	
	26		No. 2 Coy. & No. 3 Coy. on same work as above. No.1 Coy. engaged digging strong points (4) between new front and support lines in E. 22. a. 23. (Sheet 57.c N.E.) S.W. of BOURLON WOOD. No. 3 Coy. engaged on erection of apron wiring from E. 27. d. 7. 1. to E. 28. C. 5. 4. (SHEET 57.c N.E.) N.W. of GRAINCOURT (about 400 yards).	
	26/27		3 Platoons No. 4 Coy. on repair of HERMIES - GRAINCOURT ROAD. 1 Platoon " " " assisting 132nd Fd. Coy. R.E. making and keeping open overland track from CHINESE WALL to K. 14. a. 9. 5. Sheet 57.c N.E.	
	28		Nos. 1 & 2 Coys. on repair of DEMICOURT ROAD. Nos. 3 & 4 Coys. on repair of HERMIES - GRAINCOURT ROAD.	
	29.		Orders received from C.R.E. for Coys. to remain in camp in readiness for new work.	
	30/1 Dec.		Coys. 1, 2 & 3 Coys. engaged carrying up wiring material for erection of two double apron belts of wire N. of FLÉSQUIERES (RESERVE LINE).	

STRENGTH of Battalion on 1st November 1917.   41 Offrs. 789 O.R.
                                                "   40 "   944 "
                                                "   30 H

HOEUVRES SECTOR

Secret.

Army Form C. 2118.

WAR DIARY
or
INTELLIGENCE SUMMARY.

(Erase heading not required.)

November, 1917.   16th R. IR. RIFS. (P.)

Place	Date	Hour	Summary of Events and Information	Remarks and references to Appendices
			CASUALTIES during month:-	
			KILLED. DIED OF WOUNDS. WOUNDED	
	4		— — 1 (at duty)	
	20		— 1 —	
	2.		2nd Lt. E.V. BRIGGS, transferred to 12th R. IR. RIFS.	
	3.		Lt. N.D. MALCOLMSON, evacuated to ENGLAND.	
	6.		2/Lt. J.H. DOUGAN. " " "	
	10		Capt. S.W. KNOX ordered medical Board, whilst on leave to England.	
	13		2/Lt. E.W. LOGAN to England in appointment to Indian Army Reserve of officers	
			REINFORCEMENTS during month.	
	1		2/Lt. H.M. RUTLEDGE rejoined Battalion.	
	2		" N.F. IRWIN joined Battalion for duty.	
	6		2/Lts. R.F. BEVERIDGE and J.W. FURBISHER joined Battalion.	
	10		10. O.R. joined Battalion.	
	15		6 O.R. joined " "	
	20		5 " " " "	
	21		170 " " " "	
	25		6 " " " "	
	28		3 " " " "	
			GENERAL:-	
			During month parties sent to courses at:-	
			3rd Army School of Instruction	
			4th " 6 OR's " "	
			4th " " Lewis Gun School.	
			4th " " Bombing School	

1.12.1917.

J. Howard
Lt. Colonel.
Commdg. 16/R. IR. RIFS. (P.)

SECRET.

Army Form C. 2118.

WAR DIARY
of
INTELLIGENCE SUMMARY.
(Erase heading not required.)

16th R. IR. RIFLES. (P)

December 1917.

Instructions regarding War Diaries and Intelligence Summaries are contained in F.S. Regs., Part II. and the Staff Manual respectively. Title pages will be prepared in manuscript.

S/49.

WL 25

Place	Date	Hour	Summary of Events and Information	Remarks and references to Appendices
CAMBRAI FRONT.	1		Battalion engaged in section of double apron wiring N.W. FLESQUIERES.	
	2		do	
		11 A.M.	Camp occupied by Battalion South of HERMIES heavily shelled resulting in casualties: 5 killed; 22 wounded, including CAPT. O.H. MACREADY dangerously & LT. N.C. DAWSON very slightly.	57 C.W.1.d.2.9.
	3		CAPT. O.H. MACREADY died of wounds in No 29. C.C.S.	
	4	8 a.m.	Orders received that Battalion would move to DESART WOOD on this date.	
		1 p.m.	Battalion moved to DESART WOOD. No tents being available men had to sleep out all night.	
	5	11 a.m.	Orders received that Battalion would move to HAVRINCOURT WOOD to-day.	
		4 p.m.	Battalion moved to HAVRINCOURT WOOD 8.15.c. sheet 57c.	
	5/6		Battalion engaged in digging Reserve Trench W. of VILLERS PLOUCH.	
	6/7		Battalion engaged in digging Reserve trench from R.T.G. 7.2 to R.2.C.1.05 and renovating + firestepping HINDENBURG LINE from R.1.d.85.t to R.2.6.3.7. (REF. Sheet BEAUCAMP 1/10.000)	

Secret

Army Form C. 2118.

WAR DIARY
or
INTELLIGENCE SUMMARY.
(Erase heading not required.)

16th R. IR. RIFS. (P.)

December 1917.

Instructions regarding War Diaries and Intelligence Summaries are contained in F. S. Regs., Part II. and the Staff Manual respectively. Title pages will be prepared in manuscript.

Place	Date	Hour	Summary of Events and Information	Remarks and references to Appendices
CAMBRAI FRONT	7/8 to 10/11		Work of renovating D firestepping HINDENBURG LINE continued.	
	11/12		Work commenced digging new trench between R.3. b.7.1 & L.33. b.3.2. (Rg sh. BEAUCAMP.)	
	12/3		" continued, but owing to heavy shelling was stopped. Lt (A/Capt.) H.L. DICKSON and Lt. H.GREEN wounded.	
	13		Battalion camp shelled. 4 O.R. wounded.	
	13/14 to 15/16		Work on new trench continued and good progress made.	
	17		Battalion moved to camp at ETRICOURT.	
	18		" entrained at ETRICOURT, detrained at MONDICOURT and marched to SOMBRIN via SAULTY. Very heavy snowdrifts encountered. Transport moved by Road.	
	19 to 23		Battalion engaged in clearing snow drifts on SOMBRIN - GRAND RULLECOURT ROAD; SOMBRIN - WARLUZEL RD; and SOMBRIN - SAULTY ROAD	
	24		Bathing arrangements conducted in village.	
	25		Xmas Day - Rest!	

Secret

Army Form C. 2118.

16th Bn R.IR.RIFS.(P)

WAR DIARY
INTELLIGENCE SUMMARY

(Erase heading not required.)

Dec. 1917

Place	Date	Hour	Summary of Events and Information	Remarks and references to Appendices
	26		Battalion bathing	
	27		Infantry training.	
	28		do.	
	29	3.30 a.m.	Battalion moved to MOREUIL area (transport by road) entrained at MONDICOURT 9 a.m.; detrained at MOREUIL at 2 p.m. and marched to billets in HESSERES. Portion of transport detailed to proceed by rail held up in SOMBRIN by snow.	
	30		Battalion resting	
	31	2 a.m.	Transport that moved by road arrived.	
			Strength of Battalion on 31.12.1917. 43 offrs. 905 O.R.	

1.1.1918

[signature]
Lt. Colonel.
Commdg. 16th Bn. R.IR.RIFS.(P)

Secret. C/123

Army Form C. 2118.

WAR DIARY
—or—
INTELLIGENCE SUMMARY.

JANUARY 1918   16th Bn. ROYAL IRISH RIFLES. (C.P.)

Place	Date	Hour	Summary of Events and Information	Remarks and references to Appendices
	1		Battalion in MEZIERES.	
	2.3.4		Infantry training carried out.	
	4		50 O.R. sent to 15th R. IR. RIFS.	
			25 O.R. sent to 14th R. IR. RIFS.	
			26 O.R. sent to 10th R. IR. RIFS.	
	5		99 O.R. B.I. now arrived with Battalion	
	7		Battalion moved to CAIX.	
	8 to 11		Infantry training etc.	
	12		Battalion moved to CHAMPIEN.	
	13		Resting.	
	14		Battalion moved to dug outs N. of hand SERAUCOURT (S.W. ST QUENTIN)	
	15.16		Bathing.	
	17		Nos. 1 & 2 Coys. engaged on road repair at ST. SIMON.	
	18		Road repair completed.	
	19		Bn. HQ. moved into G.D. SERAUCOURT.	
			Companies started work on repairing, deepening & widening trenches	

Secret.

Army Form C. 2118.

16th Bn. R. IR. RIFS. (P)

WAR DIARY
or
INTELLIGENCE SUMMARY.
(Erase heading not required.)

Place: ST. QUENTIN FRONT

Month: January

Date	Hour	Summary of Events and Information	Remarks and references to Appendices
19		trenches as follows:- (Ref. sheet 66C. N.W. 1/20,000 FRANCE)	
		No 1 & 2 Coys. @ L'EPINE de DALLON in A.4.	
		No 3 Coy. " BOYEAU de STATION in B. 20 c.	
		No 4 Coy. " CONTESCOURT in A. 24. & A. 16 d.	
20.22		Coys. engaged on same work.	
23		No.1 Coy. joined No 4 Coy on BOYEAU de CONTESCOURT.	
24		No 4 Coy. joined No 2 Coy on strong point L'EPINE de DALLON.	
25.31		All Coys. engaged on same work.	
		STRENGTH of Battalion on 1st January 1918 43 Offrs. 903 O.R.	
		" " " " 31st " " 1918 43 " 879 "	

[signature]
Major
Commandg. 16th R. IR. RIF. (P.)

1·2·1918.

SECRET. S/60.

Army Form C. 2118.

WAR DIARY
of
INTELLIGENCE SUMMARY.
(Erase heading not required.)

16th␣ROY.␣IR.␣RIFS.␣(P.)

Instructions regarding War Diaries and Intelligence Summaries are contained in F.S. Regs., Part II. and the Staff Manual respectively. Title pages will be prepared in manuscript.

JM 27

Place	Date	Hour	Summary of Events and Information	Remarks and references to Appendices
	February 1918			
	1		Battalion worked as follows:- Hd.Qrs. GRAND SERAUCOURT.	
			Nos 1 & 2 Coys. in SOMME DUG-OUTS N. of GD. SERAUCOURT.	
			Nos. 3 & 4 Coys. in QUARRY DUG-OUTS N.E. of GD. SERAUCOURT.	
			Companies engaged on following work :-	
			No 1 Coy. in CONTESCOURT ALLEY (C.T.) Sh. 66 C.N.W. A.24.a. widening and deepening to 8' x 6' x 3', laying trenchboards, also on dug-out construction, same area.	
			Nos. 2 & 4 Coys. on construction of Strong Point - L'EPINE de DALLON.	
			No. 3 Coy. in STATION ALLEY (C.T.) Sh. 66 N.W. B.26.a. widening and deepening to 8' x 6' x 3', also laying trenchboards.	
	2 to 13		All Coys. engaged on same work.	
	14		Nos. 1, 3 & 2 & of No 4 Coy. moved into Dug.outs at JEANNE d'ARC S.P. (B.19d.B.29c.) & B. 26a). Remainder of No 4 Coy. moved into DALLON village H.10.b.)	
			B.M. H.8. & No. No 26 Coy. moved into JAMES village.	
	15-27		All Coys. on same work.	
		2.30	No 3 Coy. moved into quarters in A.26.b (S.H. 66.C)	

36th Div. Front
St. QUENTIN
SECTOR.

Army Form C. 2118.

WAR DIARY
or
INTELLIGENCE SUMMARY
(Erase heading not required.)

16th R. IR. RIFS. (P.)

February 1918.

Place	Date	Hour	Summary of Events and Information	Remarks and references to Appendices
Brulé Front St QUENTIN SECTOR	22		Half No 4 by. moved from DILLON to GIFFECOURT.	
	23		8th Sqn. moved from HAMEL to GRAND SERAUCOURT.	
			No 2 by. engaged improving new quarters	
			No 1 by. " " construction of GROUGIES S.P. H.13.a. (54. 66. N.W.1.)	
			" 3 " " " " "JEANNE d'ARC" S.P. B.19.a. B.20.c. r.c. (54. 66. N.W.1.) (das)	
			" 4 " " " " BOADICEA S.P. H.11.c. (54. 66. N.W.1.)	
	24		On this date battalion re-organised in a three company basis, in accordance with A.H.Q. O.B. 2155. of 13.2.1918 - personnel of No 4 by. being distributed over remaining bys.	
	25		No 1 by. engaged on GROUGIES S.P., No 2 by. on BOADICEA S.P. and No 3 by. on JEANNE d'ARC S.P.	
	26. 28		All bys. engaged as above.	
			STRENGTH of Battalion on 1st February 1918 43 oppo. 890. O.R.	
			" " " " " "28th" 43 " 892 "	

2. 3. 1918.

W. Allen (?)
Major ft
Command 16 R.IR. RIFS. (P.)

36th Divisional Pioneers

16th BATTALION

ROYAL IRISH RIFLES.

MARCH 1918

SECRET. S/63

Army Form C. 2118.

Instructions regarding War Diaries and Intelligence
Summaries are contained in F.S. Regs., Part II.
and the Staff Manual respectively. Title pages
will be prepared in manuscript.

WAR DIARY
or
INTELLIGENCE SUMMARY.
(Erase heading not required.)

16th Bn. Royal Irish Rifles. (P.)

March, 1918.

Place	Date	Hour	Summary of Events and Information	Remarks and references to Appendices
	1.		Battalion located as follows:- H.Qrs. GRAND SERAUCOURT. No. 1 & 3 Coys. in dug-outs JEANNE D'ARC Redoubt (B.19.d. B.20.c. & B.26.a. Sheet 66c N.W.) ½ No. 2 Coy. in shelters at A.26.b. 3.y. (Sheet 66 c. N.W.) ½ " " dug-outs at GIFFECOURT. Battalion engaged on following work:- No. 1 Coy. construction of dug-outs at GRUGIES and "BOADICEA" central (Sheet 66c N.W.) No. 2 Coy. wiring at BOADICEA and constructing elephant shelters at same place. No. 3 Coy. wiring at JEANNE D'ARC and constructing elephant shelters there, also wiring at GIFFECOURT.	
	2 to 15		All Coys. engaged on work as above.	
	16.		½ of No. 2 Coy. took over from No. 1 Coy. construction of dug-outs at BOADICEA. 1 platoon No. 3 Coy. joined No. 1 Coy. on construction of dug-outs at GRUGIES.	
	17 to 20		All Coys. on work as above.	
	21.		Battle. No. 2 & 3 Coys. concentrated to west of SOMME dug-outs N.W. GRAND SERAUCOURT. The entire of No. 1 Coy. consisting of 9 officers and 150 O.R. failed to appear at above rendezvous & having apparently been cut off at JEANNE D'ARC were subsequently posted as missing.	
		3 p.m.	Orders received from C.R.E. for two Coys. to start construction of a track for artillery near ST. SIMON. No. 2 & 3 Coys. started on this work.	
	21/22.		Battalion concentrated at OLLEZY.	
	22.	9 a.m.	Battalion moved to ESTOUILLY where instructions received from C.R.E. that Battn. would proceed to SOMMETTE EAUCOURT to construct strong points along Canal between that village and OLLEZY.	
	1 p.m.		Battalion moved to SOMMETTE EAUCOURT.	
	23.		Instructions received from 36th Divn. G. (verbal) that Battn. would be attached	

SECRET.
S/63.

Army Form C. 2118.

WAR DIARY
— of —
INTELLIGENCE SUMMARY.
(Erase heading not required.)

Instructions regarding War Diaries and Intelligence Summaries are contained in F. S. Regs., Part II. and the Staff Manual respectively. Title pages will be prepared in manuscript.

16th Bn. Royal Irish Rifles ( )   March 1918.

Place	Date	Hour	Summary of Events and Information	Remarks and references to Appendices
	23/24		Still in action, gradually retiring to line N. of VILLESELVE and in action there during the day.	
	24.	9.30 p.m.	Retired via GUISCARD to BEAULIEU.	
	25.		Moved to AVRICOURT and subsequently to WARSY.	
	26.	10 a.m.	Instructions received from 36th Divn. that Battalion would be in Divisional Reserve, along with 107th Brigade group. Lt. Col. C.F. MEARES admitted to Hospital, command of Battn. taken over by Major W.J. ALLEN.	
		12 noon.	Instructions received from 107th Brigade for Battalion to take up position between GUERBIGNY and Road Junction at Q.22 central, with right on GUERBIGNY - ERCHES Road facing north. Battalion took up this position.	
		2 p.m.	Instructions (verbal) received from Bde. Major 107th Bde. that Battalion would take up position in trenches between ERCHES and BOUCHOIR to close a gap there. These instructions were subsequently confirmed in writing and above position taken up.	
	27.	6.30 a.m.	Battalion in action, fighting very severe.	
		9 a.m.	Battalion subsequently concentrated in two groups:- (a) group under Major W.J. ALLEN to west of ARVILLERS. (b) group under Capt. J. MAXWELL to east of ARVILLERS. Orders received by "a" group to rejoin Divn. at SOURDON, with other details of 36th Divn. to "b" group attached to 30th Divn. & took up position with other details of 30th Divn. south east of ARVILLERS to protect right flank of 30th Divn.	
	28	10 a.m.	"b" group in action & subsequently moved back to SOURDON.	
	29.		"a" group moved to COURMELLE & engaged constructing strong points.	
	30.		"b" group moved to CHAUSSOY. Both parties moved to VELENNES and subsequently to SAKEUX	

SECRET.

Army Form C. 2118.

WAR DIARY
INTELLIGENCE SUMMARY.
(Erase heading not required.)

March, 1918.   16th Bn. Royal Ir. Rifles. (P.)

Place	Date	Hour	Summary of Events and Information	Remarks and references to Appendices
	31.	11 a.m.	Battalion entrained at SALEUX and proceeded to GAMACHES where it detrained and marched to OUST MAREST.	
			Strength of Battalion on 1st March, 1918. 43 offrs. 898 o.r. " " " " " 31st " " 20 " 449 "	
			Casualties during operations 21st to 31st March, 1918.	
			Killed. Died of wounds. Missing. Wounded.	
			Officers :— 2/Lt. E.E.BURNSIDE. Capt. W.H.MADDEN. Lt.(a/Capt) J.M.BAILLIE. Lt.(a/Capt) N.C.DAWSON M.C.	
			2/Lt. A.N.G.SKELLY. Lt. G.W. HINDS.	
			" D. PAUL. " T.J. WHITE.	
			" W.Q. REA. 2/Lt B. BRADY.	
			" C. HALLINAN. " F. HAYDEN.	
			" E. CROKER. " R.F. BEVERIDGE.	
			" J.H.K. FREELAND. " R. COCKS (gassed).	
			" N.F. IRWIN.	
			" J.W. FURBISHER.	
			" W.H.K. GIBSON.	
			" G.A. DAY.	

N.D. Allen
Major.
Commdg. 16th R.Ir. Rifles. (P.)

2.4.1918.

36th Divisional Pioneers

1/16th BATTALION

ROYAL IRISH RIFLES (Pioneers)

APRIL 1918.

WAR DIARY or INTELLIGENCE SUMMARY

(Erase heading not required.)

16/ R. Ir. Rifles (P.)

APRIL 1918.

Place	Date	Hour	Summary of Events and Information	Remarks and references to Appendices
	1		Battalion arrived at GAMACHES by train from SALEUX and marched to billets in OUST MAREST. Transport arrived by road.	
	2 & 3		Resting. Nothing etc.	
	4		Moved to EU and entrained there, detraining at	
	5	6 am	at REXPOEDE (Belgium) and proceeded by motor lorries to BRAKE CAMP, N. of BRANDHOEK by BRAKE CAMP.	
	6		Moved to TURCO CAMP N. of YPRES. Transport to MURAT CAMP LINES	
	7		Refitting etc.	
	8		do and Infantry training	
	9			
	10		No. 2 Coy. engaged on maintenance of ALBERTA and MOUSETRAP TRACKS & construction of alternative track.	
	11		No.3 Coy engaged on maintenance of GROUSE and GLOUSTER TRACKS & construction of alternative track. No.1 Coy — Infantry training	
	12		No. 2 & 3 Coys on above work	
			No.1 Coy commenced work under C.R.E. - Coys. on construction of Pill Boxes at OBLONG and CIVILIZATION FARMS.	
	13		Coys engaged as above. Battn. moved into PITTSBURG CAMP.	
	14		Companies engaged on reorganisation, owing to arrival of large drafts.	
	15		No. 2 & 3 Coys engaged on same work as on 12th & 13th inst. Transport moved back to CARDOEN CAMP (A 18 & 9.7 sheet 28 N.W.), leaving small detachment at MURAT LINES	
	16		No 2 Coy moved to 'SOME' CAMP adjoining CARDOEN CAMP.	
	17	11/30 pm	Transport detachment at MURAT LINES shelled, Casualties 5 killed 2 wounded.	
		½ to 1	½ Nos. 1 & 3 Coys engaged on Salvage work in TURCO CAMP. Remainder of Battn. on Infantry training.	

36th Division YPRES SECTOR

Army Form C. 2118.

WAR DIARY
or
INTELLIGENCE SUMMARY.
(Erase heading not required.)

16th Battn. R. Ir. Rifles (P.)

APRIL 1918.

Instructions regarding War Diaries and Intelligence Summaries are contained in F. S. Regs., Part II. and the Staff Manual respectively. Title pages will be prepared in manuscript.

Place	Date	Hour	Summary of Events and Information	Remarks and references to Appendices
CANAL BANK N. of YPRES.	18.		Bn. HQ. & No.1 Coy. & No.3 Coy. moved back to CARIBOU CAMP at A12 C 2.4 sheet 28 N.W. & No.1 Coy. moved into dug CANAL BANK N. of YPRES.	
	19, 20, 21		½ No.1 Coy. engaged on construction of Defence line on west of canal. Remainder of Battn. Infantry training	
	22.		½ No.2 Coy. relieved ½ No.1 Coy. in CANAL BANK and took over work on Defence line. Remainder of Battn. on Infantry training	
	23, 24, 25		Battn. engaged as above	
	26.		½ No.2 Coy. moved from CANAL BANK to SOME CAMP.	
	27.		No.2 Coy. engaged making Infantry track from CANAL BANK to ELVERDINGHE-VLAMERTINGHE RD. Shelling delayed work. Casualties 5 O.R. wounded. Remainder of Battn. on Infantry training	
	28.		No.2 Coy. completed track	
	29.		No.1, 3 Coys. engaged on construction of defence line at BRIELEN. No.2 Coy. engaged repairing roads in forward areas when damaged by shell fire	
	30.		No.1, 3 Coys. continued work on BRIELEN DEFENCES. No.2 Coy. on Infantry training	

Strength of Battalion on 1st April 1918.
" " " " 30th "

REINFORCEMENTS:
The following drafts joined Battn. during month:—

	OFFICERS	O.R.
7	-	49
12	-	320
13	-	60
23	1	-
25	-	10
28	2	6

W. Allen
Major
Commdg. 16/R. Ir. Rifles (P.)

SECRET

16TH
ROYAL IRISH RIFLES
(1/5/18)

Instructions regarding War Diaries and Intelligence Summaries are contained in F.S. Regs., Part II. and the Staff Manual respectively. Title pages will be prepared in manuscript.

Army Form C. 2118.

WAR DIARY
or
INTELLIGENCE SUMMARY.
(Erase heading not required.)

16th ROYAL IRISH RIFLES (PIONEERS)

Wt. 30

Place	Date	Hour	Summary of Events and Information	Remarks and references to Appendices
YPRES FRONT	1		Battalion located as follows:— Headquarters & No 3 Coy at "CARIBOU" CAMP. S.W. of WOESTEN (A.3.C.1.4. 28.N.W.). No 1 & 2 Coys at "SOME". (A.18.t.O.2. ").	
			Coys. engaged on following work:— No 1 Coy in BRIELEN defences, revetting, repairing duckboards, construction of tramways etc. No 2 Coy in dismantling wooden huts etc at SIEGE Camp near ELVERDINGHE. No 3 Coy repairing & improving RUM FARM RAILWAY tracks from CANAL BANK to the LAMERTINGHE–ELVERDINGHE line; dismantling huts at B.20.a.6.5 (28.N.W.) and running "RAMP" at B.27.c.6.8 (28.N.W.)	
	1.14		All coys. engaged as above.	
	15		No 2 Coy joined No 1 Coy in BRIELEN defences.	
	16.17.		No 1 & No 2 Coys took over work of dismantling huts etc from No 2 Coy.	
	18.		Coys. engaged as above. No 3 Coy started mining near SIEGE CAMP.	
	19.27.		Coys engaged as above. No 3 Coy also engaged improving RUM & BLEEN tracks and strengthening bridges to take artillery.	
	28		No 2 Coy ceased on salvage of huts etc in vicinity of CANAL BANK. No 3 Coy started work in ELVERDINGHE – LAMERTINGHE line & also on RUM FARM & tram way. No 1 & 3 Coys as before.	
	29.31		All coys engaged as above.	
			During month, drill & gym. training, bombing, signalling training was carried out. Parties were also sent to courses at Army & Corps Schools.	
			Strength of Battalion on 1st May 1918 31 offrs. 1943 O.R. " " " 1st June 1918 34 " 1630 "	33 offrs. 1943 O.R. 34 " 1630 "

Cunningham Capt.
Commanding 16/R.I.R. R.I.F.(P)

SECRET

Army Form C. 2118.

Instructions regarding War Diaries and Intelligence Summaries are contained in F.S. Regs., Part II. and the Staff Manual respectively. Title pages will be prepared in manuscript.

WAR DIARY
INTELLIGENCE SUMMARY.
(Erase heading not required.)

16th R. Ir. Rifs (P.)

JUNE 1918.

Place	Date	Hour	Summary of Events and Information	Remarks and references to Appendices
36th Div. Front YPRES SECTOR.	1.		Battalion located as follows:- HQ. No 1 and 2 Coys. SOMME CAMP (S.W. of WOESTEN - 28 N.W. A 18 d. o. 2.) No 3 Coy. CARIBOU CAMP (" " A 3 c 1.4) Transport "W" CAMP	
	2.3		Companies employed on work as follows:- No. 1 Coy. BRIELEN LINE " 2 & 3 Coys. ELVERDINGHE - VLAMERTINGHE LINE & making ALLEN TRACK suitable for Artillery use	
	4.		do do	
36th Div Corps Reserve	5.8.		HQ. No 3 Coy. and Transport moved to Camp on POPERINGHE - WATOU ROAD at L 4 b. 6.6. No 1 and 2 Coys. on POPERINGHE - PROVEN ROAD at L 4 b 2.5 No 1 Coy. engaged on BLUE LINE (EAST POPERINGHE) constructing trenches, shelters etc. " 2 " " " GREEN LINE (VLAMERTINGHE) " etc " 3 " " Infantry training Lewis Gun practice etc.	
	6		Transport moved to Lines at F 35 d 7.8.	
	9		Sunday. No work done.	
	10.		No. 3 Coy. relieved both No.1 & 2 Coys. on work. No. 1 & 2 Coys. engaged in Infantry training etc.	
	11.		Coys. employed as above. No. 1 & 8 Coys moved to Aerodrome Camp North (F.3 a 9.9) S. of PROVEN	
	12.		As above.	
	13		As above. HQ. No. 2 moved to Aerodrome Camp North No. 2 Coy. to Pigeon Camp (F.13 d. 8.8.)	
	14		No 1 & 3 Coys. relieved No 2 Coy. on GREEN and BLUE LINES respectively. No 2 Coy. on Infantry and Lewis Gun training.	
	15		As above	
	16		Sunday. No work on Defences.	
	17.		No.1 Coy. ceased work on GREEN (VLAMERTINGHE) LINE and commenced work on BLUE LINE from POPERINGHE-YPRES ROAD to RAILWAY at A 22 CENTRAL, clearing ground to 300 x in front of trench & existing wire entanglement No 2 & 3 Coys as before.	

WAR DIARY
INTELLIGENCE SUMMARY

Army Form C. 2118.

16th R. Ir. Rifs. (P.)

JUNE 1918.

Place	Date	Hour	Summary of Events and Information	Remarks and references to Appendices
	18-22.		As above	
	23.		Sunday. No work. Church parades only.	
	24-25.		As before	
	26		No. 3 Coy. relieved No. 2 Coy. on above work. No. 2 Coy. on Infantry training etc.	
	27		No. 1 Coy. as before. do	
	28.		No. 2 Coy. proceeded to ROUBROUCK for musketry Firing practice. No. 1 & 3 Coys. on work as before.	
	29-30.		do do	
			During the month specialist training in Lewis Gun, Bombing Signalling were carried out.	
			Strength of Battalion on 1st June — 32 Officers 1034 O.R.
			do do 30th " 32 " 1084 "
			Casualties :— Nil. 1 O.R.	

1-7-18

[signature] Lt. Colonel
Comdg. 16th R. Ir. Rifs. (P.)

SECRET.

Army Form C. 2118.

WAR DIARY
~~INTELLIGENCE SUMMARY~~
(Erase heading not required.)

16th (S) Bn. Royal Irish Rifles (Pioneers).

Vol 3 2

July, 1918.

Instructions regarding War Diaries and Intelligence Summaries are contained in F.S. Regs., Part II. and the Staff Manual respectively. Title pages will be prepared in manuscript.

Place	Date	Hour	Summary of Events and Information	Remarks and references to Appendices
II Corps Reserve. PROVEN.	1.		Battn. located as follows:— H.Q., No 1 & 3 Coys : Aerodrome Camp N. (Ref. Sheet 27 – F.13.a.9.9.) No 2 Coy : Pigeon Camp. (" " – F.13.b.8.8.) Transport. (" " – F.25.d.7.8.)	
	2.		Coys. employed as follows:— No 1 & 3 Coys: Work on Blue (E. Poperinghe) Line. Wiring & clearing field of fire in front of trench. No 2 Coy.: Firing musketry practice at Roubrouck.	
	3.		Work proceeded as above:— Battn. moved to Road Camp. No 2 Coy. rejoining Bn. from Roubrouck.	
XVI French Corps Reserve.	4.		Battn. moved into Billets near St Silvestre Cappel. Locations H.Q.: P.33.a.9.1. No 2 Coy: P.35.b.6.2. Transpt: P.35.d.9.2. No 1 " : P.28.c.7.3. " 3 " : P.35.c.7.1.	
St Marie Cappel Area.	5–6.		Cleaning Billets. Inspections etc.	
	7.		Infantry Training – Specialist Training in Lewis Gun, Signalling & Bombing.	
II Corps St Jans Cappel Sector	8.		100 men each of Nos 2 & 3 Coys. moved to Billets S.E. of Mont Des Cats – No 2 Coy: R.27.d.6.8. – No 3 Coy: R.21.c.0.4. Forward ½ No 2 Coy. engaged on work at R.22.b. – Constructing C.T.'s Wiring etc. Rear ½ Coy – Infantry Training. " " " 3 " " " " " R. 21. d., R. 33. b., R. 27. c. – Mine'd dug-out construction, deepening & revetting trenches, completing M/G. emplacements. Wiring. Rear ½ Coy. Infantry Training	
	9–18.		As above.	
	16.		Transport moved to line at P.33.a. 5.6.	
	19.		Forward ½ Coy. No 2 Coy. moved to Posts at Mont Noir– M. 19. d. 8. 2. Rear ½ No 3 Coy. joined forward ½ Coy. at Mont Des Cats.	
	20.		No 1 Coy. as before.	
	21.		Forward ½ No 2 Coy. engaged on work connected with posts garrisoned by them. No 3 Coy. on work as before. No 1 Coy. moved to Fiebrouck – R. 27. a. 4. 7.	
	22.		Work proceeded as before as regards No 2 Coy. & ½ No 3 Coy. Remainder No 3 Coy. & whole of No 1 Coy. employed wiring Trench digging & cutting down crops at X.4.d.	

Army Form C. 2118.

WAR DIARY
or
INTELLIGENCE SUMMARY.
(Erase heading not required.)

Instructions regarding War Diaries and Intelligence Summaries are contained in F.S. Regs., Part II. and the Staff Manual respectively. Title pages will be prepared in manuscript.

Place	Date	Hour	Summary of Events and Information	Remarks and references to Appendices
ST JANS CAPPEL SECTOR.	23.		Work as above. Rear ½ No 2 Coy. moved to PIEBROUCK for work with No 1 Coy.	
	24.		Mont Noir Posts heavily shelled with Gas, night 23/24th. 1 Officer 28 ORs. Wounded-Gas. No 1 Coy works also shelled - 10HV 1 OR Wounded	
	25-28		Work as before. Night of 25th part of No 3 Coy. shelled out of billets. 1 OR. Wounded	
	29.		½ No 2 Coy. at PIEBROUCK employed on road repairs at BERTHEN - R.27.a. Remainder as before.	
	30.		No 1 Coy. employed on road repairs - FONTAINE - BERTHEN - ROSSIGNOL - CANTA CORNER - STAINES HOUSE ROAD - R.17.c, R.23.b & R.24.a. No 2 Coy (MONT NOIR) & No 3 Coy. as before.	
			½ No 2 Coy. (PIEBROUCK) - Road Screening.	
			Strength of Battn. 1st July. 32 Officers 1087 ORs	
			— do — 31st July. 33 " 1054 "	
			Casualties during month. Wounded 1 Off. & 3 ORs.	
			" Gas " 1 " x 32 "	

W. Allen
Lieut. Col.
Commandg. 16th R. Ir. Rifles. (P.)

1st August, 1918.

36th Divn. G SECRET.

Herewith War Diary of this
Battalion for the month of August, 1918.

L.C. Brown
Lt. & Adjt.
for Lieut. Colonel
Comdg. 16th R. Ir. Rifs.
(P.)

SECRET
Army Form C. 2118.

Vol 33

WAR DIARY

Instructions regarding War Diaries and Intelligence Summaries are contained in F.S. Regs., Part II. and the Staff Manual respectively. Title pages will be prepared in manuscript.

INTELLIGENCE SUMMARY. 16th Bn. Royal Irish Rifles (Pioneers).

August, 1918. (Erase heading not required.)

Place	Date	Hour	Summary of Events and Information	Remarks and references to Appendices
ST JANS CAPPEL SECTOR.	1.		Battn. located as follows: Bn. H.Q. 27/P. 33. a. 9. 1. No. 3 Coy. R. 21. c. 0. 4. No. 1 Coy. R. 27. a. 4. 7. Transport P. 33. a. 5. 6. ½ No. 2 Coy. M. 19. d. 8. 2. " " R. 27. a. 4. 7. Companies employed on following work:- No. 1 Coy: Repair & maintenance of Roads: FONTAINE - BERTHEN. BERTHEN - SCHNESCHEN. ROSSIGNOL - CANTA CORNER. ROSSIGNOL - BERTHEN. PIEBROUCK. STAINES HOUSE ROAD. ½ Platoon No. 2 Coy: Providing garrison of posts at MONT NOIR M. 19. d. 8. 2. Revetting & improving same posts. Constructing shelters & dug-outs for garrison. No. 3 Coy: Construction of mixed dug-out for M.D.S. at R. 20. d. 1. 7. & for Brigade H.Q. Deepening & duckboarding trenches & wiring at X. 4. d. - R. 35. c. (BLUE LINE) ½ Platoon No. 2 Coy: Road screening at R. 17. c., R. 16. c., R. 14. b., R. 20. a., (NEAR BERTHEN)	
	2-12.		Work proceeded as above.	
	3.		Battn. H.Q. moved to ARAN COTTAGES - R. 13. C. 8. 1. (Gr MONT DES CATS)	
	8.		Owing to shelling of Billets No. 3 Coy. had to dig in. Shelters constructed in bank etc. at R. 20. d. 8. 6. (near BERTHEN)	
	10.		2 Platoons No. 2 Coy. located in billets at R. 27. a. 4. 7. moved to billets at R. 25. 35. to relieve congestion.	
	12.		2 Platoons No. 1 Coy. moved to billets at R. 14. b. 4. 6. to relieve congestion & to avoid shelling. No. 3 Coy. carried work on M.D.S. dug out & commenced work on trenches (Deepening, duckboarding etc.) at R. 34. d.- X. 5. a. & X. 10. b. Other Coys remained on work as above.	
	13.20.		Work proceeded as above.	
	21.22.		Battn. co-operated with Infy. in a minor operation for the capture of NURAL & WIRRAL FARMS; being employed to erect a single wire fence from X. 17. a. 3. to S. 8. d. 2. 5. in front of newly captured line. Work about ⅔ do completed. Casualties 8 o.R. wounded.	
	22.23.		During the progress of operation Battn. was engaged in slight fighting resulting in the capture of an enemy machine gun. Work proceeded as on 20. 21.st	
	23.24.		No 3 Coy. & No 1 Coy. employed to dig new front line trench from X. 17. av. 55. 60 to X. 17. b. 60. 60. Casualties 3 o.R. wounded 2 o.R. killed. No 2 Coy. carried on work as on 20/21.st (N.W. of BAILLEUL)	

T2134. Wt. W7708—776. 500000. 4/15. Sir J.C. & S.

SECRET.

Army Form C. 2118.

WAR DIARY
of
INTELLIGENCE SUMMARY. 16th Bn. Royal Irish Rifles. (P.)

August, 1918. (Erase heading not required.)

Instructions regarding War Diaries and Intelligence Summaries are contained in F.S. Regs., Part II. and the Staff Manual respectively. Title pages will be prepared in manuscript.

Place	Date	Hour	Summary of Events and Information	Remarks and references to Appendices
	24.25.		Work continued - whole Batt. (less 2 platoons at Mont Noir) digging front line trench from X.17.f. 60.65. — X.12.c.75.30.	(N. and N.W. of Bailleul)
	25.26.		Batt. employed wiring new line captured by left Bde. Wire fence erected from S.9.a.6.9. — S.3.d.5.5. x about 100 yds at S.8.c.8.8. One Coy. unable to do any work owing to non supply of material, arrangements for which were made by Bde.	
	26.27.		Wiring in S.8.c. x a. continued	(N. & NW of BAILLEUL)
	27.28.		No work done.	
	28.29.		No. 1 & 3 Coys. employed digging front line for left Bde. sector - S.6.6. – S.7.c. & S.3.d. total 600 x. ½ No. 2 Coy wiring front line S.8.c.x.	
	29.30.		No. 1 & 3 Coys continued digging new front line - 800 yds. S.3.d. – S.9.a.	
	31.		Coys employed opening up & repairing roads radiating from St JANS CAPPEL towards BAILLEUL ASSUM &c following withdrawal of enemy. MONT NOIR posts abolished. Bn. moved to St JANS CAPPEL. H.Q. established at x.6.a. 55.95. Transport lines at R.21.a.6.2.	
			Strength of Battn. 1st August. 33 Offrs. 1048 O.R.	
			31st " 36 " 1022 "	
			Casualties during month. Killed. Wounded. W.d. Gas	
			2 OR. 18 OR. 2/Lt. T. BROWN. 22/8.	

P.S. 207
1.9.1916.

W Allen Lieut. Col.
Commdg. 16th Bn. R. Ir. Rifles. (P.)

SECRET

Army Form C. 2118.

Vol 34

WAR DIARY
INTELLIGENCE SUMMARY

16th Bn Royal Irish Rifles (Pioneers)

September 1918

Instructions regarding War Diaries and Intelligence Summaries are contained in F.S. Regs, Part II. and the Staff Manual respectively. Title pages will be prepared in manuscript.

Place	Date	Hour	Summary of Events and Information	Remarks and references to Appendices
	1		Battalion located in ST JANS CAPPEL. Battalion H.Q. at X 6 a. 55-95. Transport at R.21a.6.2. (near BERTHEN)	
			Battalion employed opening up and repairing roads between ST. JANS CAPPEL, CROIX DE POPERINGHE and BAILLEUL, in the neighbourhood of the ASYLUM. Roads badly pitted with shell holes. Littered with fallen horses +etc	
	2		Road repair continued. Transport lines moved to ST JANS CAPPEL at S.1.E.1.7	
	3		do do do	
	4		do do Battalion working on the BAILLEUL – RAVELSBERG Road as far as CRUCIFIX CORNER (S.18.a.6.2)	
	5		do do do	
	6		No 1 & 2 Coys Bathing. No 3 Coy repairing road S.E of ST JANS CAPPEL – Ca DE POPERINGHE (S.2.C.29 – S.2.a.8.5 – M.32.d.9.7.)	
	7		2 Platoons No 3 Coy continued working on same road as yesterday. Remainder of Battn working on RAVELSBERG Road from CRUCIFIX CORNER. E. NEUVE EGLISE (S.18.a.6.2. – T.14.b.4.0)	
	8		Battn continued work on RAVELSBERG – NEUVE EGLISE Road. Weather very wet + stormy rendering roads in very bad condition	
	9		Battn moved to S.18.a. 20.65 near CRUCIFIX CORNER. Men dug in in Banks in Jesses & No work done on this day in consequence	
	10		Repair of RAVELSBERG – NEUVE EGLISE ROAD continued – roads in very bad condition due to heavy rain. Transport moved to S.11a. 2.0. Men had to dig in. Also	
	11		Work continued as yesterday – much hampered by heavy rains. Drains dug in sides of roads	
	12		No 1 Coy commenced work on road from S.11.a.4.1 (NEERSEBROM) towards BAILLEUL passing MAGILLIGAN CAMP. (S.9.d.7.0) Road in very bad condition. No 3 Coy bathed in evening	
			Nos 2 + 3 Coys continued on NEUVE EGLISE – RAVELSBERG ROAD	

Army Form C. 2118.

WAR DIARY
or
INTELLIGENCE SUMMARY.
(Erase heading not required.)

September Cont.

Place	Date	Hour	Summary of Events and Information	Remarks and references to Appendices
	13		Work continued - Still raining heavily	
	14-15		Same work continued - Weather improved and work accelerated	
	16		No 2 Coy commenced work on road from S.17.C.7.8 - S.11a.14.1. (Road junction with RAVELSBERG ROAD. TO MEERSEBROUK) Nos 1 & 3 Coys continued on same roads as before	
	17-19		Work proceeded as on 16th - No 1 Coy constructed a drain and culvert.	
	Night 19/20		Battalion moved to GODEWAERSVELDE - 27/Q.18.a.7.9. (Billets in empty houses)	
	20-21		Spent resting, cleaning equipment	
	Night 21/22		Battalion moved to Huts & Tents near HOUTKERQUE (27/E.20.a - SHRINE CAMP)	
	22		Resting & cleaning up generally.	
	23		Battalion moved to Nissen Huts at Camps at 27/F.14.c.5.9. on PROVEN - POPERINGHE ROAD Transport at 27/F.14.a.3.5.	
	24		Coy spent repairing and fixing up huts (erected from salved material and in bad condition)	
	25		Work commenced erecting huts in MIDDLESEX & COUTNOVE & CAMPS. F.14.c.0.5. and F.14.d.2.2. (100 men each of Nos 2 & 3 Coys.) No 1 Coy training	
			No 2 & 3 Coy carried on same work. No 1 Coy commenced dismantling Road screening on CROMBEKE ROAD from CATERPILLAR CORNER to INTERNATIONAL CORNER, and on ST JANS TER BIEZEN - POPERINGHE ROAD	
	26-27		Work carried on. Battalion bathed and clothes fumigated. Parties left work for this purpose returning subsequently	
	28		Battalion in readiness to move all day. Move to YPRES ASYLUM (28/H.7.a.5.5) effected about midnight	
	29		Transport moved to REIGERSBURG CAMP locality (28/H.6.a.5.8). Battalion occupied in obtaining cover for billets &c	
	30		Work commenced on repair of roads in neighbourhood of BLACK WATCH CORNER (28/J.15.a)	

Army Form C. 2118.

WAR DIARY
INTELLIGENCE SUMMARY.
(Erase heading not required.)

Place	Date	Hour	Summary of Events and Information	Remarks and references to Appendices
September (cont^d)			During the month 50 O.R. of Reception Camps were transferred to 2nd Battⁿ Q.V.Rif^s (19.9.18) Also 100 men were attached to 105th and 110th Field Ambulances for work as additional Stretcher Bearers during the Advance (28.9.18)	
			Strength of Battⁿ 1st September 1918 36 Off^s 1022 O.R.	
			30th September 1918 37 Off^s 1020 O.R.	
			Casualties during month — Nil.	
			Wallan Lieut Colonel	
			Commdg 16th K.R. du Rifles (P)=	
2nd October 1918				

SECRET.

Operation Order No. 26.

Ref. Map. Sheet. No. 1/40,000.

1. Battalion less Transport will concentrate at "C" Camp this afternoon at 5-15 p.m.

2. ORDER.   Bn. H.Q., "D", "C", "B", and "A" Coy.

3. Will pass starting point - X Roads (/A.   ) at 5-45 p.m. - proceeding via DANISH CROSS.

4. Usual Distances between Companies.

5. "B" Coy. will detail N.C.O. to report Bde. H.qrs. at "C" Camp for allotment of concentration ground.

6. Billets to be cleaned up at once and left in a sanitary condition. Usual certificates will be forwarded to this Office.

7. ACKNOWLEDGE.

(Sgd) C.L.CAZLUX. Capt. & Adjt.
10th(S)Bn. The Royal Irish Rifles

Copies to :-
107th Infantry Brigade.
Commanding Officer.
All Companies.
Quartermaster.
Transport Officer.
R.S.M.
File.

Army Form C. 2118.

WAR DIARY
or
INTELLIGENCE SUMMARY.
(Erase heading not required.)

1/5 Royal Irish Rifles (Pioneer)   Vol 35

Instructions regarding War Diaries and Intelligence Summaries are contained in F. S. Regs., Part II. and the Staff Manual respectively. Title pages will be prepared in manuscript.

October 1918

Place	Date	Hour	Summary of Events and Information	Remarks and references to Appendices
	1		Battalion moved from YPRES ASYLUM to near BECELAERE (Sheet 28 - J.12.c.5.3.) Advanced Transport consisting of Coy. Tool wagons, S.A.A. & Lewis Gun Limbers, Cookers & nil Batte. Remainder of Transport and Q.M. Stores at H.6.a.5.8 (near REIGERSBURG CAMP.) Battalion dug in and in bivouac.	
	2-3		Battalion employed on repairing road from ZONNE BEKE - BECELAERE. A party of about 60 men were sent to the 108 Fd Ambulance as Additional Stretcher Bearers.	
	4		Work continued down to junction of road with MENIN - YPRES road. No. 2 Coy continued work on road from BECELAERE southwards. On night of 4/5 No. 1 and 3 Coys wired about 1200 yds of the front line from L.19.a.9.3. to L.19.a.13. Party shelled on Roosey rd. "L/S. Dunwoody being killed and 4 men wounded. Rear Transport moved to near POTIJZE - 28 I.4a. 9.3.	
	5		No. 2 Coy employed as above 50 men each of No. 1 and 3 Coy. employed at night carrying T.M. Ammunition up to front line. 1 N.C.O. killed and 2 wounded	
	6		All Coys employed as before. Nos. 1 & 2 Coy on BECELAERE - ZONNE BEKE rd. No. 3 Coy on BECELAERE - DADIZEELE road.	
	7-11		All Coys. employed on repairing road from BECELAERE@DADIZEELE as far as TERHAND.	
	12.		Rear Transport & Q.M. Stores moved forward to J.12.C.4.4. Two Officers, five N.C.O's & ten men from each company billets and dry/airy.	
	13.		Working line from L.13.6.50.46 to L.13.d.10.90 and thence to L.19.c.20.80 on night of 12/13. Battalion (without right of Tunnel 138-142. battalion dug junction of tunnel 3 day. 2.6" wide). Casualties from M.G. fire, one man died of wounds 72 men wounded (62 Coy)	

Army Form C. 2118.

WAR DIARY
or
INTELLIGENCE SUMMARY.
(Erase heading not required.)

16th Bn. Royal Irish Rifles (Pioneers)

October 1918.

Instructions regarding War Diaries and Intelligence Summaries are contained in F. S. Regs., Part II. and the Staff Manual respectively. Title pages will be prepared in manuscript.

Place	Date	Hour	Summary of Events and Information	Remarks and references to Appendices
	14.		Div. attack. No 3. Coy moved off 08:30 to KEZELBERG CROSS RDS E.19.d.40.80. & filled in craters, made road passable for all arms. Bivouacd L.19.d.	
	15.		Hqrs, 1 & 2 Coys moved off 09:30 to K.17.a.6.4. 1 & 2 Coys Repair Tramway Track & Opened metal on TERHAND – VIJWEGEN Road.	
			No 1 & 2 Coys with rations from DADIZEELE HOEK to GOLDEN CROSS RDS. No 3. Coy finish craters at KEZELBERG CROSS RDS & fill shell holes. Casualties, one man of No 3. wounded.	
			On DADIZEELE – KEZELBERG Rd. Bn. Hdqrs moved in convoy to GRAN En L.15. at central transport. S. M. Abric moved to K.17.d.6.4.	
	16.		Battn. on burial work in Divis. Area. working from LEDEGHEM – MENIN Rly forward. Battn moved in evening, Hdqrs to L.11.c.7.9.	
			Transport & Companies & 8. p.m. above to L.11.a. Billets in farm houses.	
	17.		Battn on burial work. Casualties – two men of Battn wounded in their billet by enemy shell.	105 GR's gone from ADMS Sadafejuy
	18.		No 1. Coy remain & carry on burial & salvage. No 2 Coy move to A.15.c.6.4. East of WINKEL ST. ELOI. Hqrs at A.15.d.3.5.	
	19.		No 2. Coy on maintenance & repair of WINKEL ST. ELOI – LENDELEDE Rd from Ruyenia A.21.a.40.05 to A.18.c.6.5. inclusive.	
			No 3. Coy. inspection & cleaning of billets. No 1. Coy. Carry on Salvage work till afternoon when they rejoined Battn & located in A.14.c.	
	20.		No 1. Left a. Coy on LENDELEDE – HULSTE Rd from A.18.C.6.5. to Cross roads at B.20.c.6.9.5. No 2. Left Coy. On Road from B.20.c.9.5.6	
			HULSTE B.22.c.4.3. No 2. Right Coy on WINKEL ST. ELOI – LENDELEDE Rd from	
	21.		No 1 & 3 Coys move off at 08:30 to LYS CANAL to assist R.E's in bridging. No 2 works B.24.c.1.14 & 2 on B. C.19.9.7.3. Work from 09:00 till 16:00 at night.	
	22.		No 2. Coy as on previous day.	
	23.		Hdqrs, Q.M. Stores & No 2. Coy move to E. of HULSTE. Hdqrs located B.23.d.9.8. Tanspt. B.23.d.4.7. No 2. Coy attached to 121 Fd Coy R.E. for work. Casualties – one man of No 1. Coy wounded. Hdqrs, No 2 Coy & part of transport issued a change of clothing. Clean clothing issued for Nos 1 & 3.	

A6945 Wt. W14422/M1160 350,000 12/16 D.D. & L. Forms/C/2118/14.

Army Form C. 2118.

WAR DIARY
or
INTELLIGENCE SUMMARY.

16th Roy Irish Rifles (Pioneers)

(Erase heading not required.)

Instructions regarding War Diaries and Intelligence Summaries are contained in F.S. Regs., Part II. and the Staff Manual respectively. Title pages will be prepared in manuscript.

Title pages October 1918.

Place	Date	Hour	Summary of Events and Information	Remarks and references to Appendices
	23.		On bridges over LYS. 30 O.R.'s of No.2 Coy. attached to 110 Fd. Amb. for Cholera work. No.1 Coy assisting in bridging. No. 3 Coy	
	24.		Repairing road approach & making a corduroy road C.14. C.6.0 to C.13.a.central.	
			No.1 Coy assisting R.E.'s in bridging B.24 & C.10. No.2 Coy repairing road C.19. No.3 Coy Bridge approaches C.14 central & maintaining	
			Road C.14. C.6.0 — C.13.a. central.	
	25.		No.1 Coy road repairs C. 20.a.11 — C. 20.a. Central to C. 26. B. 5.3 to C. 27. c. 37. No 2. Coy on approaches to bridge. C.19. 6. 6.7.	
			No.3. Coy. on road repairs C.20.c.2.8. — C.27.c.3.7. — I.3. a. 5.8 — I.3.d.1.0. and filled craters at L.5. & 9.6. 2 I.O.R's of No 1. Rpnt to 110 Fd. Amb. for Cholera work	
			No.1. Coy on road repairs I.3. Central — I.9. d.10.50. No.2. Coy bridge approaches C.19.6.0.7. No.3 Coy road repairs. C. 27.C.3.7. I.3.a. 5.8.	
	26.		I.3.a.1.0. & crate filled at C. 26.6.7.6. 22 O.R's guard from D.R.C.	
	27.		No work. Coys. clean up. 50 O.R.'s relieve from 110 Fd. Amb.	
	28.		Batn. moved at 11:30 to LENDELEDE. Billeted in the town.	
	29.		Batn. moved at 08:10 under orders of 108 Bgde. Route — B.26.d.8.8 — H.14. BISSEGHEM — Bridge at M.5.C.2.2. — MARCKE — AELBEKE	
			to MOUSCRON. Move completed at 16:00. Billeted in the town. 3 Coys at S.16.C.74. H.Qrs at 8.16.a.2.3. Received by G.O.C. en route.	
	30.		Coys clean up; fix up billets with water. Transport moves to factory at S.15.a.6.4.	
	31.		Batn. on railway work; No.1 Coy clearing destroyed track & repairing formation S.17 & 28; No 2. Coy filling mine craters in	
			formation 1 mile N.E. of STERNHOEK HALTE; No 3 Coy clearing and condemning S.17.	

T.J.134. Wt. W708—776. 500000. 4/15. Sir J. C. & S.

Army Form C. 2118.

WAR DIARY
or
INTELLIGENCE SUMMARY.
(Erase heading not required.)

Army Form C. 2118.

October 1918   16th Royal Irish Rifles (Pioneers)

Place	Date	Hour	Summary of Events and Information	Remarks and references to Appendices
			Casualties during October	
			2/Lieut Dunwoody S. killed 5.10.18	
			2 Other Ranks killed	
			14 - Do - Wounded	
			Strength	
			1st October 37 Officers 1020 O.R.	
			31st October 35 " 961 "	
			[signature] H. Allen	
			Lieut Col	
			Commdg 16th Royal Irish Rifles (P)	

Army Form C. 2118.

WAR DIARY
or
INTELLIGENCE SUMMARY.
(Erase heading not required.)

16th R. W. Rifles (Pioneer).

November, 1918.

Place	Date	Hour	Summary of Events and Information	Remarks and references to Appendices
MOUSCRON (Sheet 29/S.22)	1.		Battn. located in MOUSCRON being billeted in the town. Employed on Railway Work. No 1 Coy. lifting track in S.28 and C.(Sheet 29) No 2 Coy filling mine craters, No 3 Coy. clearing a demolished bridge in S.17. Work detailed by the 8th C.R.T.	36
	2-4		General work as above continued on the Railway.	
	5		Work continued - Battalion bathed and all blankets disinfested.	
	6-9		Work carried on as above.	
AUTRYVE (29/V.8.d)	10		Battalion moved at 5.30 a.m. to AUTRYVE (Sheet 29 V.8.d) for work on Bridges over SCHELDT under orders of C.E. X Corps. Work commenced at 6.30 p.m. by No 1 & 2 Coys. Men working in shifts at AUTRYVE (Sheet 29/V.8.d) BOSSUIT (Y.13 central) and ESCANAPPLES (V.10.d)	
	11-12		Work of repairing approaches to Bridges, filling in craters, building ramps to continued.	
	13		No 1 Company not out at work. Company inspected by C.O. in full equipment.	
	14		Battalion H.Q. inspected by C.O.	
	16		No 2 Compy. not out at work - inspected by C.O.	
MOUSCRON (29/S.22)	18		Battalion moved to MOUSCRON, occupying same billets as at beginning of month. Marched off at 8 a.m.	
	19		Bn. bathed, blankets & services dress fumigated. Afternoon - Kit inspections.	
	20.		Infantry Training. Conference held at Battn. H.Q. to discuss questions of Training. Education, Sports &c. It was decided to form Committee to undertake supervision of Education, Athletics & make suggestions as to what should be done for the welfare of the men.	

T2134. Wt. W708-778. 500000. 4/15. Sir J. C. & S.

Army Form C. 2118.

WAR DIARY
or
INTELLIGENCE SUMMARY.
(Erase heading not required.)

Instructions regarding War Diaries and Intelligence Summaries are contained in F.S. Regs., Part II. and the Staff Manual respectively. Title pages will be prepared in manuscript.

Place	Date	Hour	Summary of Events and Information	Remarks and references to Appendices
	21		Training and sports programme continued.	
	22.		Companies route marching in morning - Football in afternoon.	
	23		Inspections &c in morning - no work in afternoon.	
	24		Church parade only.	
	25.26		Infy. Training. general drill to each morning. Platoon Football league commenced. A class for all illiterate men was started on 25th a room in the convent being fitted up as schoolroom. Attendance about 40 + men appeared keen to learn. Arrangements in charge of chaplain. These men who were teachers in civil life.	
	27th		Battalion carried out a Route March. - accompanied by Transport. Route Sheet 29 LUIGNE (S24). PETIT VOISINAGE (S19)- TOMBROEK (S14) M31 a.3.6. - M29 d.4.2 - S17 d.2.2. - Billets.	
	28-29.		Infantry Training and sports.	
	30.		Battalion bathing. Inspections &c. During the latter part of the month one platoon was engaged drawing German beds from ROUBAIX. These are made in sections, & were fitted up in the convent. Each man has his own bed. Paillasses were also drawn & men made as comfortable as possible.	
			Strength. 1st Nov. 1918. 35 Officers 959 OR. 30th Nov. 1918. 35 Officers 947 OR.	

J. C. Boynton Major.
Comdg. 16th R. Ir. Rifles (P)

Army Form C. 2118.

WAR DIARY
or
INTELLIGENCE SUMMARY.

(Erase heading not required.)

Army Form C. 2118.

16th R. IRISH RIFLES (P.) (Secret.)

December 1918

Instructions regarding War Diaries and Intelligence Summaries are contained in F.S. Regs., Part II and the Staff Manual respectively. Title pages will be prepared in manuscript.

Place	Date	Hour	Summary of Events and Information	Remarks and references to Appendices
MOUSCRON	1		Church Parade. Bn located in billets at MOUSCRON and engaged in Educational Schemes, Sports, Drill etc	
"	2		Bn Ceremonial Parade on Football ground MOUSCRON in preparation for Divisional Parade to be held on 3rd inst	
"	3–5		Divisional Parade on 3rd inst cancelled. Capt Pearson takes over duties as Bn Education Officer from Capt Loyd. C.F. Mahenahis & Arithmetic classes commenced. Want of accommodation & proper materials cause some difficulties which are however overcome, and all ranks were keen to learn. Classes took place in Convent in class room specially fitted up.	
"	6		Divisional Ceremonial Parade held at HALLUIN AERODROME. Bn marched from quarters at 0730 hrs returned for lunch at 13.30. Conference at Bn Hd Qrs to consider catering for Men's Xmas Dinner	
"	7		Bn bathing. Football in afternoon. Capt Knox assumes command of Bn vice Major Colquhoun D.S.O. on leave.	
"	8		Church Parades.	
"	9		Two Elementary French Classes commenced and one advanced class. Good attendance especially from No 1 Coy.	
"	10		Training, Sports & education continued. Afternoons still devoted to sports games etc	
"	11		Training etc continued. First draft of Coalminers including the R.S.M. proceeded to United Kingdom for demobilisation	
"	12, 13		Sanitary improvements completed in Convent Yard. All ranks at this period quite comfortable	
"	14		Bn bathed. Sports in afternoon and football match Officers v N.C.Os (draw)	
"	15		Training continued. 12 W.Os & N.C.Os sent to Regtl Depot BELFAST for release as "War Worn"	
"	16		Divisional Review Parade before 15th Corps Commdr. at 1100 hrs. Morning wet cold and stormy Men steady on Parade and marched back well. Returned to Convent at 13.30 hrs.	
"	17		Second Conference held at Bn Hd Qrs respecting Men's Xmas fare. It was decided to rely on Divl Canteen for supplies. Drawing of German beds from ROUBAIX completed & discontinued	
"	18		Military, Athletic and Educational Programme continued	

Army Form C. 2118.

WAR DIARY
or
INTELLIGENCE SUMMARY.
(Erase heading not required.)

Dec. (Contd)

Place	Date	Hour	Summary of Events and Information	Remarks and references to Appendices
MOUSCRON	19		Bathing day	
"	20-24		Preparations for Xmas. Bn Male Voice Choir formed under Bugle Major assisted by 2/Lt Beveridge. 24th was granted as holiday to No1 Co.	
"	25		Xmas Day & Boxing Day holidays. Church parade in morning. Dinner served from 12:30 hrs - 1300 hrs. All visited by C.O. Excellent meal arranged by Q.M. Canteen Officer and Bn Cooks. Abundance in food and drink to our great content and "All Merrie"	
"	26		No1 Coy proceeded to new quarters at LE BLANC FOUR for urgent work on light Railways under 235th L.R. Forward Coy R.E. Coy left at 1100 hrs.	
"	27-28		Training continued for remainder of Bn. Bn Educational Classes move to 40 Rue de Leopold to vacant Belgian School. All conveniences at hand. School develops. Shorthand class making good progress. Men very keen to learn. School attendance numbers 150-170 [Attendance of No1 Coy excluded]	
"	29-31		Training & sports continued. Demobilization of Miners, demobilizers & pivotal men from this Bn completed.	

Strength on 1st December 1918   35 Officers   948   O.R.
"   "   31st   "   1918   35 Officers   906   O.R.

D. McLean
Lieut. Colonel
Comdg. 16th R. Irish Rifles (P.)

2/1/19

Group 1.   107th Infantry Brigade

Education Return.

1st Bn. Royal Irish Rifles.

A.

Column 1.	Column 2.
English Mathematics Writing (Elem).	30.
-do- -do- (Interm).	105.
-do- -do- (Adv).	12.
Book Keeping.	15.
Shorthand.	22.
French (O.R's).	
-do- (Officers).	

B.

Column 1.	Column 2.	Column 3.
Common fallacies in regard to demand and supply of labour.	4.	150.
Forms of government: Our own parliamentary system.	4.	

C.D.E.

Nil.

2nd Bn. Royal Irish Rifles.

A.

Column 1.	Column 2.
General Education (Elem).	13.
Commercial Eng. and Arith.	18.
French.	29.
Carpentry.	14.
Tailoring.	3.
Shoemaking.	6.
Horse Management.	12.
Farriery.	1.
Bricklaying.	2.
Chemistry.	1.

B.C.D.E.

Nil.

App II

107th Bde No. G 489.

Headquarters,
36th Division 'G'.

      Herewith please find attached monthly Education return of this Group.

      The outstanding feature in reviewing the month's work is the continued progress made by the Illiterates class who are now at a stage equivalent to 3rd standard in an elementary school.

      There has been a falling off in numbers attending at several of the classes during the latter half of the month; this was found to be largely due to Demobilisation.

      The Spanish class inaugurated during the month has proved very successful. It was found necessary to engage a civilian teacher, no other instructor being available.
      His fee (60 francs per week - 6 lessons) was defrayed by subscriptions from the officers attending the course.

      Several new classes have been formed during the period:-

    <u>36th Divl. Signal Coy. R.E.</u>

        1. Building Construction.
        2. Wireless Telegraphy.

    <u>Under Group arrangements.</u>

        1. Arabic.
        2. Spanish.
        3. Shakespeare.
        4. Latin and Greek.
        5. Carpentry (O.R's).
        6.   -do-   (Officers).

(Signed) P. Leveson Gower
Brig-General,
Commanding 107th Infty Brigade.

28.1.1919.

WAR DIARY
INTELLIGENCE SUMMARY

Army Form C. 2118.

16th (S. Bn. Royal Irish Rifles (P)

JANUARY 1919.

Place	Date	Hour	Summary of Events and Information	Remarks and references to Appendices
MOUSCRON (BELGIUM) (Sheet 29/S.22)			Battalion (less No. 1 Coy.) billeted in MOUSCRON. No. 1 Coy. billeted at BLANC FOUR (Sheet 28/X.19.b) and employed on repair work &c. on the Light Railway System, under direction of 235 L.R. Forward Coy. R.E., in neighbourhood of LINSELLES (28/N.22) and near TOURCOING (36/F.8 + F.1). No. 2 & 3 Coys. engaged in training - Military, Athletic and Educational. During the early part of the month 2½ hours each morning were devoted to Military Drill, 1 hour to Physical Drill, and the whole afternoon to Athletic Sport. Schemes for improving the education of the men were drawn up, this taking precedence over everything else. Men with no education were given systematic teaching in English and Arithmetic, including reading, writing, simple composition, elementary arithmetic &c. More educated men received instruction in Civics, Mathematics, etc. Shorthand, French and Book-keeping classes were also organised. The Battalion was fortunate in having certificated teachers in their number, and the men have greatly profited by their instruction. Many men attended Trade and Technical classes. On the 13th Coy. 1 Coy. at BLANC FOUR. Military exercises were reduced to 1 hour Arms Drill and 2 hours Physical Drill and Tactical Exercises each day.	

Army Form C. 2118.

WAR DIARY
or
INTELLIGENCE SUMMARY.
(Erase heading not required.)

Place	Date	Hour	Summary of Events and Information	Remarks and references to Appendices
			Sports were regularly organised. Football both Rugby & Soccer, cross country running, Tug-o-War, & Basket Ball being the chief games. Demobilisation proceeded more rapidly, men being demobilised, including Miners and men with Guaranteed offer of Employment from pre-war employers; a few long-service men were also released.	
			Strength 1st January 1919. 35 Officers 903 O.R.	
			" 31st " " 31 Officers 713 O.R.	
	1-2-19		H.J. Allen
Lieut-Colonel.
Commanding 16th R. Irish Rifles (P)	

Army Form C. 2118.

WAR DIARY
INTELLIGENCE SUMMARY.
(Erase heading not required.)

16ᵗʰ R. IRISH RIFLES (P.) Vol 39

February 1919.

Place	Date	Hour	Summary of Events and Information	Remarks and references to Appendices
MOUSCRON BELGIUM.	1		Battn. HQ. No. 1 and 3 Coys. and transport billeted in billets at MOUSCRON. No. 2 Coy. billeted at BLANC FOUR (28/x19f) and employed on work under 235 Lt. Railway forward Coy. R.E. repairing and re-opening the light Railway system in the neighbourhood of TOURCOING (36/F.8. & F.1.)	
	4		No. 1 & 3 Coys. were engaged in a military training programme and the Educational scheme adopted last month. Demobilization proceeded steadily and considerably hindered progress however. No. 3 Coy re-inforced No. 2 Coy at BLANC FOUR the latter Coy having been considerably depleted by demobilization.	
	14.		Owing to demobilization of Staff personnel no. Nos. 2 & 3 Coys were amalgamated into one Coy. under command of Capt. W.R. White M.C. The working party continuing to be found in spite of	
	15.		During the week ended this date the number of men demobilized was 783 with the week nearest the abandonment of the Educational Scheme in this week.	
	25.		6 Offrs - 205 O.R. transferred to 12ᵗʰ R. I. Rif. R.G.s for service in the Army of Occupation. Off. and men prior to this date to find sufficient personnel to form a working party still installed in MOUSCRON.	
	28.		Remnants of Nos. 2 & 3 Coys - 2 Offrs + 28 O.R. rejoined Battalion in MOUSCRON.	
			During the month 6 Offrs. 390 O.R. and 15 horses were demobilized. Strength 1ˢᵗ February 1919 29 Offrs. 694 O.R. 23ʳᵈ " " 16 Offrs. 124 O.R.	

[Signature]
Comdg. 16ᵗʰ R. Irish Rifles (P.)
Lt. Colonel

Army Form C. 2118.

WAR DIARY
~~INTELLIGENCE SUMMARY.~~
(Erase heading not required.)

16ᵀᴴ Royal Irish Rifles (Pioneers)

MARCH 1919.

Vol 4

Place	Date	Hour	Summary of Events and Information	Remarks and references to Appendices
MOUSCRON. BELGIUM.	1		Battalion billeted in MOUSCRON — being practically reduced to CADRE strength.	
	31.		Battalion billeted in MOUSCRON all the month. Reduced to Cadre strength. During the month 5 officers, 55 O.R's and 49 animals were demobilised. Strength 1st March 16 officers 111 O.R. " 31. " 8 " 46 " "	

W. Allen Lt. Col.
Commanding 16th R. Irish Rifles (P.)

Army Form C. 2118.

WAR DIARY
or
INTELLIGENCE SUMMARY.

(Erase heading not required.)   16th ROYAL IRISH RIFLES.

APRIL, 1919.

Instructions regarding War Diaries and Intelligence Summaries are contained in F.S. Regs., Part II. and the Staff Manual respectively. Title pages will be prepared in manuscript.

Place	Date	Hour	Summary of Events and Information	Remarks and references to Appendices
MOUSCRON, BELGIUM.			Battalion located at MOUSCRON pending orders for embarkation to U.K. to take home. Regimental Equipment. Battalion down to Cadre Strength. Sports were arranged under Divisional auspices and trips to places of interest organised. The first party for this Unit going to BRUSSELS on 29th April, 1919.	
			Strength 1.4.19 — 8 Officers 44 O.R.	
			do. 30.4.19 — 6 Officers 41 O.R.	

J. C. Oppenheim Major.
Comdg. 16 R. Irish Rifles (1).

www.ingramcontent.com/pod-product-compliance
Lightning Source LLC
Chambersburg PA
CBHW081551160426
43191CB00011B/1893